SALT

BUTTER

BONES

NICOLE PISANI

SALT
BUTTER
BONES

MASTERING THE ART OF
GOOD COOKING

SEVEN DIALS

To Manon,
This book is dedicated to you – you showed me that life is
solely about being happy (and eating good food)

CONTENTS

INTRODUCTION

Taste... Salt is greatly underrated
Flavour... Butter is the food of the gods
Essence... Bones are the essence of everything

EMMA CANNON

I have been cooking for most of my adult life, and before that I watched others cooking from a corner of the kitchen in my family's restaurant. I think I am now old enough to understand that there are some things you just have to accept as predetermined in life, and being involved with food and becoming a chef was clearly always written into my destiny. Over many years I have cooked in different countries with different chefs and this book is a collection of the memories and recipes that have all come together over that time and which stay with me even today.

The main purpose of any cookbook, in my opinion, is to share recipes and cooking techniques that work and that you can enjoy at home, cooked on a barbecue out near the sea, eaten alone as a treat after a long day, or with friends and family around a table when you want to feast. I hope you will be surprised at how easy some cooking techniques really are, and I want to share with you the magic of discovery and connection you can find when cooking and eating food together.

I currently work in a primary school in Hackney, East London. I started there making school lunches and now I give cooking lessons three times a week to the children. Seeing the awe in their faces as we do simple things like whisking and grating reminds me of where I want to be as a chef at this present moment. I made this choice to work here because I needed less of the intensity and striving for perfection that came with the restaurant industry and instead I wanted to pursue more of the giving to others of what I have learned about food. Every person I meet says how lucky the children are to have this opportunity to learn to cook, but really I feel I am the lucky one to be able to share this with them.

Before I joined the school, I cooked in a number of restaurants at chef de partie level, which simply means that you have a section you are in charge of and at every service you try to have the precise same movements and accuracy in your cooking. You obsess over having the same place for everything and the same timings throughout the day – I always say it's like a dance that happens between yourself and the food you cook in your space in the kitchen. Cooking the same three or four dishes throughout your shift, aiming for a consistently high standard, is the kind of cooking that is very different to how I cook at home, although there are some fundamental basics which I believe are

helpful. For example, being organised at the start and keeping a clean kitchen while cooking helps you concentrate on the food you are preparing and be mindful of the process. Having a little section in your fridge of dressings and sauces that you can dip into throughout the week when you arrive home hungry means that you can add flavour in an instant to the simplest of meals. Prep, or preparation, is everything for a good service and even at home I use my weekend to prep for a good week of easy dinners.

In most of my recipes I try to use everyday ingredients but sometimes I introduce a few lesser-known ones, like koji, for example, and techniques such as smoking foods on the hob. For me, cooking is not only a comfort but allows me to take steps out of my comfort zone, too, in the routine of how I cook or how I shop or forage for food – whether that's foraging in the woods, by the sea or on my computer sourcing things online.

I hope to go a little further in this book than just giving you a series of recipes that you can follow, so that you might use these as a canvas to create your own recipes. Once you know how to cook a rib-eye steak so that you have that seared-on-the-outside, tender-in-the-middle and no blood on the plate result every time, you can then try all kinds of finishing butters to add the extra layer of flavour – from nori to salmon to bone marrow. Having this basic skill opens up a world of different dishes. I hope that I may create possibilities for you, while also sharing with you some tried-and-tested recipes that I love, and demonstrating some techniques that serve me well.

SALT

I was born in Malta, a small island in the Southern Mediterranean positioned between Sicily and North Africa. During the summers the heat becomes thick and heavy and so every day our only relief from it was to jump into the blue crystal sea. I remember my cousin chasing us with octopus, turning the beak to spray us with its ink and my dad eating live rizzi (sea urchins) straight from the rock. I was about seven when I became obsessed with seeing salt crystalise on the rocks in shallow waters, making the light shimmer off it into a thousand colours. I remember licking it and liking the taste. We used to spend all day in the sea – maybe that is why I salt constantly while I cook.

I know salt causes debate amongst cooks and chefs. To me, the argument for and against salting after cooking is interesting because some say it is the first taste that the tongue registers, and too much can prevent the authentic flavours of the dish shining through. My belief is that salt helps rather than hinders and cooking is mostly about preference and instinct, so I guess I believe in being in tune with the idea that there is no wrong or right approach. Saying all of that, I strongly stand by having a good salt in your kitchen, one that you can use regularly and can become familiar with its strength and how much of it is needed. Maldon is one of the best salts you will find and I also like to experiment with the beautiful pink Himalayan salt, black salt from Hawaii or the wood-smoked salt which is popular in Scandinavia.

I salt at the beginning, the middle and the end of preparing a meal. If the balance of seasoning in a dish is wrong, it doesn't matter how amazingly well cooked the rest of the ingredients are, I will feel that something is missing.

I also love to brine meat (which is basically soaking it in either a salt and water or salt and sugar mix) and I recently started to brine vegetables. I would know I was going to have a good service on the meat or fish section when I salted both sides of the flesh before it hit the grill or plancha each time for every order. After resting and brushing a beautiful piece of meat with butter and carving and salting it, you tap into a feeling that you've finished something perfectly every time.

BUTTER

Butter just brings everything together. A rib-eye steak is transformed by that last basting of butter from the pan and scattering of salt flakes. On a week night I might have noodles just with cabbage sautéed in butter and topped with an egg. At barbecues I love serving sides of Jersey new potatoes in melting nori butter and a corn on the cob dipped in ginger butter.

At Nopi, a London restaurant where I worked, we used to get through 25 kilos of butter every week – each section has three or four containers of butter cut into tiny cubes per service and most dishes are finished with butter. It would arrive in blocks of 5 kilos which would then need to be cut into perfect equal-sized squares without it melting.

I remember being given a bowl of pasta with rizzi butter (sea urchin) as a child and it being just as normal as a soft-boiled egg with soldiers. This is the food I was brought up on and it was what I thought was common. I didn't realise how lucky I was to be introduced to such beautiful ingredients at a young age.

I noticed recently that many restaurants have stopped serving buttered toast at breakfast, so if you then ask for butter it will come straight from the fridge so that it doesn't have a chance of melting on the toast. I'm with Anna (Anna Hansen from The Modern Pantry) who used to give morning briefings to the whole kitchen team saying all we had to do each morning was to serve perfectly buttered toast and perfect porridge and the rest would flow from there.

BONES

Somehow I understand that bones are the essence. Bones take us back to basics, where fillets of fish are not an option. If steak tartare with an egg yolk is on the menu, it is mine. I served bone marrow in our restaurant before I even knew that you needed a special fork to be able to reach in and get it out. We had some puzzled looks from our customers! I remember learning how to cook ox cheek, very slowly, over what seemed like days, and I fell in love. When I was served a fish head on a stick at Noma, in Copenhagen, it was the perfect dish. This is what I want to say with food.

Having cooked most of my life, I realise I have cooked with instinct most of the time, with emotional intelligence when managing a team and with all my senses, regardless of what mood I am in. I can touch a piece of meat or hear a sound and know it has been or is being seared well, and I can smell when something is ready. My body clock is a cooking clock – sometimes I will rely on a timer but most days my cooking skills are my senses, and on those days I am strong.

GLOSSARY OF TECHNIQUES

I used to be a little embarrassed by all the terminology used in restaurant kitchens. Now I realise it is so helpful and I have watched friends and family grow in confidence in the kitchen with just a little more know-how.

Caramelise
Everything that contains sugar can be caramelised. This is one of the most important techniques you can learn. Duck skin is perfect when caramelised well, as is fish skin, sweet potatoes, pulses, spices and onions mostly all the time – it gives them a sweet flavour and a beautiful glaze.

Chiffonade
To slice into very thin strips or shreds. Literally translated from the French meaning 'made of rags'.

Deglaze
This is a technique to maximise the flavour in your dish by using liquid to bring together all the flavours in the pan. The pan needs to be very hot, so that once a little liquid such as wine or balsamic vinegar is added, the flavours in the pan are immediately absorbed into the liquid and the meat or vegetables or grains then immediately absorb those flavours too as the liquid evaporates.

Dice/Brunoise
To cut food into tiny cubes.

Gravalax
Meaning 'to bury', this is a Nordic word and technique which is usually used to cure salmon. The fish is buried in sugar and salt and left to cure.

Let rest
We had this idea that only meat needed to rest – basically you leave roasted meat to relax after cooking before slicing or eating, to allow the flesh to tenderise and also release any blood, which will not look good on the plate. However, my discovery is that mostly anything tastes better after resting, even soups before blitzing, and pulses are even better after being 'rested' overnight – especially curries and dhal.

Mise en place
Literally means 'set in place' – everything has a place. This is the best state of mind to be in when cooking anywhere. I normally set myself a container packed with tasting spoons and fill the sink with soap and water to wash them as I go. Keeping a clean and clear surface and having a good mise en place is what makes cooking fun and hassle-free.

Monte
This is when you continuously coat your food in a hot pan with foaming butter, using a spoon to give it a shine and a beautiful end taste. This, to me, is one of the most important things you can do in the kitchen as a chef.

Quenelle
This is a technique used to create an elegant oval, egg-shaped scoop, usually of ice cream or cream. It's really hard to explain in words so I would recommend watching an online video, but basically you use a curved spoon, heated up in water if you are quenelling ice cream, scooping first under and then curving over.

Sealing off
Sealing off meat, fish or vegetables is a fundamental cooking technique where you cook at a high temperature to create colour on the outside. It doesn't actually 'seal in' flavour as often thought, but there is specific flavour in the darker colour. This is why I love to have a grill pan (with ridges), especially for meat and grilled vegetables.

THE BEGINNING: STOCKS

One of my favourite books is *Instructions to the Cook* by Bernard Glassman & Rick Fields. The reason I love it is for all the metaphors about cooking and life:

'For the Zen cook, a seed of doubt, a pinch of faith, and a dollop of determination is enough to begin.'

My own little metaphor is that stock is the beginning of cooking, just as a good heart is for life. They are both really all you need to start with and you can work your way from there.

As a chef, the first thing I do in honour of wasting less is to always have home-made stock. I remember the words of a larger-than-life Scottish chef who ran the kitchen in my first job at The Hilton in Malta; he said to me, 'the stock is everything. Use your imagination, let it run wild, add spices, balsamic vinegars, alcohol or herbs'. That was 15 years ago and ever since I have never made the same stock twice. I make it on the hob or in the oven, and old vegetables always get transformed into fragrant stock for soups, or for simmering grains in, or poaching some fish.

You can be as adventurous as you dare with your stock. I once stayed at a silent retreat in Bali where we were able to boil up teas using an amazing variety of herbs, roots and spices; for example, turmeric root, kaffir lime or Szechuan peppercorns, which I realised could all be infused with basic vegetables to create wonderful flavoured stocks.

When you try anything for the first time, you have no clue what will happen but hopefully you want to try anyway, just to see the result. This puts off a lot of people in the kitchen, worried about the finished dish before they have put anything in the pot. But really, the beginner's mind is the best, not knowing what alchemy might happen is much more interesting than knowing for sure. Start off by simply keeping all your vegetable trimmings or meat, chicken or fish carcasses and boiling them up for a wonderfully nutritious homemade stock which can be stored in the fridge or freezer for a dish that demands it. As you become more confident with making stock, you can experiment with different flavour combinations.

I have included some recipes in this first chapter for basic stocks, and give examples of how I use them in my cooking. Often in cookery books the stock chapter is separated from everything else, but in the daily life of a kitchen it is an integral part of so many dishes.

VEG STOCK

You don't have to have celery or carrots or even onion to make a vegetable stock, although these are the classics. I love to see what flavours come from the different veg we have on hand: an end of a leek with some fennel trimmings is the start of a delicious delicate soup. (Don't use potato peelings, though, as they will turn your stock 'paste like'.)

MAKES JUST UNDER 1L

a handful of carrot peelings
celery butts
leek tops
knob of fresh root ginger,
    bruised with a knife
1 garlic clove
1 bay leaf
1 litre water
good pinch of sea salt

Add all the ingredients, except the salt, to a large saucepan, bring to the boil and then reduce to a simmer and cook for about 30 minutes.

Add salt to taste, cool and strain into a sterilised jar (see page 37 for instructions) and keep in the fridge for 4–5 days.

BABY VEG BRAISED IN SAFFRON STOCK

Baby veg is so beautiful and it is so tender that you hardly need to cook it. However, it does come with quite a lot of grit, so to really appreciate it you do have to appreciate the cleaning!

SERVES 4 AS A SIDE

pinch of saffron threads
400ml veg stock (see recipe
    opposite), warmed
250g your favourite baby veg,
    for example courgettes,
    breakfast radishes, carrots,
    turnips and kohlrabi (peeled)

Soak the saffron threads in your simple vegetable stock, add the baby veg and braise on a simmer for 8–10 minutes.

You can serve the veg in the broth as a colourful side dish for sharing if you like; it would go very well with Chicken on the Rack (page 144), Sea Bream and Mung Kitchari (page 154) or the Calves' Liver with Sage Butter (page 150) recipes.

CHICKEN STOCK

As with the veg stock, having a jar of chicken stock in the fridge gives you so many ways to add a depth of flavour to your everyday cooking.

It isn't particularly revolutionary for me to include a recipe for roast chicken, or the chicken stock that I make after we have roasted a chicken, but then again, when I am in the supermarket I always notice how many people buy skinless chicken breasts versus whole chickens, and so miss out on so much flavour. So I hope you will forgive me including these simple dishes because I think every time I cook a whole chicken it makes me happy to see how many dishes I can make from the one bird.

I feel that going for ingredients which are organic, combined with using a quality ceramic pot, makes for a beautiful stock.

MAKES APPROX. 1L

1 leftover chicken carcass
    (any size is fine)
2 roasted shallot skins, or
    2 halved raw shallots
4 garlic cloves, smashed with
    the flat side of a knife
a thumb-sized piece of fresh
    root ginger, peeled and
    roughly sliced
2 bay leaves, torn

I have included a roast chicken recipe in the chapter 'At the end of the day' (page 144) as it's so easy it doesn't need to be confined to Sunday lunch. We will often eat a leg each, then carve and pull off the rest of the meat to keep for a salad, soup or risotto over the coming days. The carcass then just goes straight into a large pot with a couple of the roasted shallot skins from the meal, some garlic and ginger and a couple of bay leaves, if we happen to have them.

Then we just cover the carcass with water, bring to the boil and reduce to a low simmer for a couple of hours, skimming away any impurities from the top. When it is done, we strain the stock through a sieve into a sterilised jar (see instruction on page 37). It keeps for up to 3 days in the fridge, or you can freeze it.

CHICKEN STOCK RISOTTO WITH ANISE HYSSOP AND BABY KALE TEMPURA

You can use many different types of grain with this simple dish to get different textures. I have used a simple short grain rice that turns out very similar to the traditional Italian Arborio risotto rice when cooked. Buckwheat, bulgur and barley are good if you wish for more of a broth.

The tempura made from anise hyssop and baby kale add a wonderful crunch to the dish, but are optional extras. Tempura is a lovely light batter which just coats the herbs, and once dropped into hot oil they only take a few seconds to puff up and crisp. I tend to buy unusual herbs for my cooking from online ingredient sellers, but I also came across anise hyssop in our local garden centre, available both in pots and seeds.

SERVES 4

For the risotto
knob of butter
2 shallots, finely chopped
2 garlic cloves, finely chopped
400g short grain or Arborio
    risotto rice
300–400ml hot chicken stock
4 egg yolks, optional

*For the anise hyssop and baby
    kale tempura*
250ml sparkling water
handful of ice cubes
100g tempura flour
500–750ml vegetable oil
200g mixed anise hyssop and
    baby kale leaves

Parmigiano Reggiano, to serve

Start the risotto. Melt the butter in a saucepan and add the shallots and garlic. Cook until soft and translucent and then add the rice to seal off (see Glossary, page 14). Stir, to make sure all the grains are coated, and cook for a minute before adding a ladleful of hot stock. Bring this to a low simmer, stirring every now and then, and adding the stock in small amounts as you go, until the rice is cooked but still with a little bite. It isn't easy to describe the best consistency for risotto; it's soft rather than stodgy, perfect for a wide-bottomed bowl.

When the risotto is ready I like to stir through 1 egg yolk per person, which cooks in the residual heat, as in a carbonara.

For the tempura batter, add the water and ice cubes to a mixing bowl. Mix in the flour until you have a consistency that is thick enough to coat the leaves well without being heavy.

If you have a deep-fat fryer, heat the oil to 180°C. Alternatively, you can half-fill a wok with vegetable oil and heat it to 180°C, using a cooking thermometer to check the temperature.

Coat a few leaves at a time in the flour mixture and carefully place them into the hot oil using tongs. If you are using the wok method, for extra safety lower the heat when placing the leaves into the oil to prevent it spitting, then bring the oil back up to temperature when you have removed one batch. Repeat with all the leaves. (Once the oil is cool you can strain it and put it back into a bottle to use once more.)

Spoon the risotto into bowls and grate over plenty of Parmigiano Reggiano. Top with the tempura and serve immediately.

BASIC SHELLFISH STOCK

As with bones, there is so much flavour in the shells of shellfish it is worth taking a little time to make a stock with these that you can use either in a bisque soup or to make the most incredible pasta dishes. My favourites are to use either crab or langoustine.

MAKES APPROX. 1L

1 whole crab shell (fresh meat
    picked) or 1kg cooked
    and discarded prawn or
    langoustine shells
1 onion, quartered
2 celery sticks, roughly
    chopped,
head of fennel, sliced
1 leek, roughly chopped
1 lemon, quartered
1 garlic clove
2 bay leaves
1 tsp black peppercorns
sprig of thyme
1 tsp sea salt

If using crab, ask your fishmonger for a freshly cooked whole crab. Pick the meat, discarding the top shell and the feathery cones (these are the lungs, which are the only toxic part of the crab).

Place the picked shell, legs and claws (or prawn shells) into a large saucepan and add the rest of the stock ingredients. Cover with water, bring to the boil, then reduce the heat to a simmer and leave uncovered for 1 hour, skimming away any white foam that comes to the top. Taste, and if you prefer a stronger flavour, simmer for another 20 minutes. Cool a little and strain through a fine sieve.

It keeps for up to 3 days in the fridge, or you can freeze it.

SEAWEED CONSOMMÉ

A consommé is a clear liquid which has the essence of the main ingredient. Here I have used seaweed, but other examples would include chicken or tomato. The clarity is obtained by using egg whites, which attract all the impurities so they can be simply skimmed off the surface before straining the liquid. Making a consommé is a bit time consuming, but the results really are beautiful, so if you are having a dinner party or making a special meal, offering a consommé definitely shows how much you care. I was lucky enough to visit the restaurant Locavore, in Bali, where the early courses that weren't even on the tasting menu were quite stunning, all made with local Balinese ingredients. They served a tomato consommé with tomato sorbet as a cleanser and it really was so clean. It was one of the best moments of the evening.

I like to use kombu, which is a type of seaweed that is becoming more readily available in the Asian sections of supermarkets, online or in health food or Asian shops.

MAKES 1.5L

3 small sheets of kombu seaweed
2 dried shiitake mushrooms
a thumb-sized piece of fresh root ginger, peeled
8 kaffir lime leaves
1 celery stick, roughly chopped
5 egg whites, whisked (keep the yolks for curing, page 61, or to make mayo, page 58), optional

Add the kombu sheets to a large pan of water, approximately 2 litres, along with the shiitake mushrooms, ginger, kaffir lime leaves and celery. Bring to the boil and add the whisked egg whites, if using. (It is absolutely fine to not follow this step – you will still have a lovely broth – this is for when you really desire the clarity of a consommé.)

Simmer gently for 1 hour. The egg whites, if using, will form a solid crust on top of the broth, which helps to clarify the stock. Remove from the heat and allow to rest before passing the liquid through a muslin-lined sieve. Discard the solids.

It keeps for up to 3 days in the fridge, or you can freeze it.

CRAB STOCK BROTH WITH CRAB TOAST

Often the most flavoursome parts of shellfish are thrown away. For example, there is so much intense flavour in the head of the prawn or the crab shell. When you make a stock or broth from these parts, it is extremely nourishing.

SERVES 4

800ml crab stock (page 26)
2 egg whites (keep the yolks to make homemade mayo, see page 58)
meat from the crab
2 tsp sesame oil
1 tbsp cornflour
2 tbsp light soy sauce
2 tbsp finely chopped coriander leaves
2cm piece of fresh root ginger, grated
2 garlic cloves, finely chopped
4 slices sourdough
4 tsp sesame seeds

Heat the crab stock in a saucepan over a medium heat.

Meanwhile, whisk the egg whites to a foam and mix together with the crab meat, sesame oil, cornflour, soy sauce, coriander, ginger and garlic.

Toast the sourdough slices under a hot grill – fully on one side and lightly on the other. Spread the crab mixture over the lightly toasted sides, sprinkle over the sesame seeds and grill for about 6 minutes. Serve the broth in bowls with the crab toasts alongside.

LANGOUSTINE SPAGHETTI

I have included this recipe in the stock section as it is so dependent on the bisque – in other words, the stock. Scottish langoustine are equally delicious boiled or grilled. In this recipe I simply boil them until just cooked, peel them carefully to keep as much of the meat as possible, then use the pile of shells to make a deep, flavourful bisque-based sauce for the fresh spaghetti, keeping back a couple of whole langoustines for each serving.

SERVES 4 (plus leftovers)

800g raw Scottish langoustines
1 tbsp unsalted butter
1 small onion, roughly chopped
1 celery stick, chopped
1/2 fennel bulb, roughly
    chopped
1/2 thumb-sized piece of fresh
    root ginger, roughly sliced
pinch of chilli flakes
1 tsp peppercorns (pink or black)
200ml Pernod
500ml just-boiled water
400ml tin coconut milk
400g dried spaghetti
sea salt

Bring a large pan of water, along with a couple of heaped teaspoons of sea salt (enough to make the water as salty as the sea) to the boil. Add the langoustines and boil for 2–3 minutes until the flesh is no longer translucent. You may need to boil them in batches, as it's important not to crowd the pot.

Drain the langoustines, refresh under cold running water and set aside one or two for each serving. When cool to the touch, remove the heads of the rest and squeeze the shell so that you can easily peel them. Chill the peeled langoustines and keep the heads and shells to make a bisque sauce.

Melt the butter in a large saucepan over a medium heat and soften the onion, celery and fennel for a few minutes before adding the ginger, chilli flakes, peppercorns and the langoustine heads and shells. After another minute or so, deglaze (see Glossary, page 14) the pan with the Pernod before adding the just-boiled water, bring back to the boil, then lower to a gentle simmer for about 1 hour until the liquid has reduced by half, removing any impurities that come to the surface with a slotted spoon. Stir in the coconut paste, and taste for seasoning.

Bring another pan of water to the boil and add the spaghetti, give a stir and reduce the heat a little to a good simmer until the pasta is cooked, usually 5–6 minutes. Drain and return to the pan.

Stir the langoustine bisque into the pasta until all the strands are evenly coated. Serve topped with the whole langoustines (which have been waiting at room temperature).

FRIDGE & LARDER LOVE

For a chef, preparation is at the heart of every successful dish. When I am cooking at home, what I have already to hand makes the difference between an easy or a hard life. As soon as you arrive home hungry, having a few condiments or pickles helps you on the way to a wholesome supper. For example, once I have pickled some onions I will add them to a steak salad, dhal or even an egg sandwich.

INFUSED OILS, VINEGARS & SALTS

I have an old cordial bottle which has become one of my best cooking friends since I first filled it with extra virgin olive oil, then added a mix of bashed cardamom pods, nori flakes, a black garlic clove, a few bay leaves and lavender, gave it a good shake and let it infuse for a couple of weeks. I didn't know it would be so good but it instantly lifted a salad and is perfect to drizzle over burrata or labneh when I have friends round. Having ready prepared infused oils gives you a speedy way to finish dishes with flavour; they provide that little touch which, without wishing to sound over the top, elevates the most simple of dishes. As with pickling or making spice mixes, infusing oils is just a case of trying what you fancy and seeing what happens. I use medium-quality extra virgin olive oil as I'm adding flavour and a really quality olive oil needs nothing extra. There is no set 'use-by' date for these oils, provided they are stored properly in a cupboard (rather than on the counter top), and for me they even improve with time.

SIMPLE STERILISATION METHOD

It's important to use really clean jars for any oils, vinegars and pickling to prevent mould. A simple way to sterilise them is just with hot water. Place your jars in the sink, pour in just-boiled water up to the top so that it is just running over the sides. Once the water is cool enough to touch, pour away and leave the jars to air dry.

CITRUS-INFUSED OIL

MAKES 500ML

500ml extra virgin olive oil
Pared zest of 1 lemon/orange

Place the extra virgin olive oil in a pan with the pared zest. Gently warm for 5 minutes. Allow the oil to cool before transferring to a sterilised airtight jar (see above).

CARDAMOM-INFUSED OIL

MAKES 500ML

500ml of extra virgin olive oil
5 cardamom pods, cracked
   open
2 sprigs of fresh lavender,
   rinsed and dried
peel of 1 orange
2 star anise

Put all the infusing ingredients into the bottle of extra virgin olive oil. Shake and allow to infuse in a cool dark place for at least a couple of weeks before using.

ROSEMARY-INFUSED OIL

MAKES 500ML

500ml extra virgin olive oil
50g fresh rosemary, picked
   and chopped
2 garlic cloves, smashed,
   peeled and chopped

In a small saucepan over medium-low heat, heat 1 tbsp of the olive oil and gently fry the rosemary and garlic for three minutes. Allow to cool and add to the rest of the olive oil, transferring to a sterilised, airtight jar or bottle (page 37). Give a good shake and allow to infuse, ideally for a couple of weeks before using.

MUSTARD-INFUSED OIL

MAKES 500ML

500ml extra virgin olive oil
3 tbsp mustard seeds

Place the extra virgin olive oil in a pan with the mustard seeds. Gently warm for 5 minutes. Allow the oil to cool before transferring to a sterilised, airtight jar (page 37).

ELDERFLOWER VINEGAR

We were given some elderflower vinegar by Claire Ford at Borough Market, in London. I had to ask for the recipe as it has such a taste of spring. You'll need access to an elderberry shrub or tree; look out for the delicate white elderflower blossoms to appear (round about June), snip off a few of the flower heads, give them a rinse and shake off any bugs. Alternatively you can buy them from specialists online.

MAKES 500ML

a few white elderflower
    blossoms
500ml white wine vinegar

Place your washed elderflowers in a sterilised 500ml glass jar. Pour over the white wine vinegar and leave to infuse for a couple of weeks before straining through a sieve lined with muslin or cheesecloth into a fresh sterilised, airtight jar (page 37).

INFUSED SALT

MAKES ABOUT 70G

70g sea salt
1 tsp of rosemary sprigs/lemon
    peel/any flavour you like

Just as you can infuse olive oil with flavours, so you can for salt, too. Add your flavour to the salt, mix well and store in a sterilised, airtight jar (page 37). Taste after a couple of weeks and you should have a lovely flavour.

PICKLING & FERMENTING

When summer comes around in Malta, with its strong heat, we try to find ways to make things last forever, or at least throughout the year. The idea of preserving foods is now very fashionable in restaurant kitchens all over the world. Our grandmothers in Malta used to go down to the beach with a simple picnic of pickled vegetables and squashed tomatoes to pile between slices of bread (hence including the Giardiniera recipe (page 47), while in Japan the traditional way of keeping vegetables uses a bacteria called natto, which not only preserves them but adds another layer of flavour.

PICKLED SEAWEED

MAKES 150G

25g dried seaweed, soaked in
    water (150g soaked weight)
400ml apple cider vinegar
200ml water
50g coconut sugar
1 tsp cumin seeds

Add the soaked seaweed to a sterilised, airtight jar (page 37). Add the apple cider vinegar, water, coconut sugar and cumin seeds to a pan and bring to the boil. Pour this hot liquid over the seaweed. Allow to cool to room temperature, close the jar and keep in the fridge for up to 6 weeks.

When serving, slice into julienne strips, and use as 'pickles on the side' for rice dishes, with salad or fish dishes.

PICKLED MUSTARD SEEDS

MAKES APPROX. 400G

200g yellow mustard seeds
300ml apple cider vinegar
150g sugar
100ml water
2 kaffir lime leaves

Place the seeds in a warmed sterilised, airtight jar (page 37). Heat the apple cider vinegar, sugar, water and kaffir lime leaves in a saucepan until boiling, then pour the liquid over the seeds. Allow to cool to room temperature, close the jar and keep in the fridge for up to 6 weeks.

Add to dressings, using the liquid as part of the dressing along with the pickled seeds, and any cooked or raw vegetables you fancy.

PICKLED RED ONIONS

MAKES 700G

1–2 red onions, sliced
400ml red wine vinegar
50ml lemon or lime juice
1 heaped tbsp coconut sugar
1 tsp mustard seeds

Add the onions to a sterilised, airtight jar (page 37). In a saucepan, bring the apple cider vinegar, lemon or lime juice up to the boil, add the coconut sugar and mustard seeds, stir until the sugar has dissolved and pour over the sliced onions. Allow to cool to room temperature, fasten the lid and refrigerate for up to 2 weeks (leave at least for a day and you will see them turn an amazing colour).

PICKLED CHERRIES

MAKES APPROX. 1KG

500g cherries, stems and
    stones intact
500ml red wine vinegar
100g sugar
1½ tbsp sea salt
1 tsp Szechuan peppercorns
3 cinnamon sticks
3 bay leaves
3 star anise
1 tsp cloves
1 tsp fennel seeds

Place the cherries in a sterilised, airtight jar (page 37). Bring the remaining ingredients up to the boil in a saucepan, reduce to a simmer until the sugar has dissolved, then pour over the cherries. Allow to cool to room temperature, then fasten the lid and refrigerate for up to 2 weeks.

PICKLED RADISHES

MAKES APPROX. 600G

200g radishes, washed and
    sliced thinly (with a mandolin
    or sharp knife)
300ml Champagne (or white
    wine vinegar)
50g sea salt
50g sugar
2 tsp caraway seeds
10 sprigs of dill

Place the radishes in a sterilised, airtight jar (page 37).

In a saucepan, bring the Champagne (or vinegar) up to the boil.
Add the salt, sugar and caraway seeds, then stir until the sugar has
dissolved.

Pour over the radishes and add the dill, stirring into the liquid. Allow
to cool to room temperature, fasten the lid and refrigerate for up to
2 weeks.

PICKLED DANDELION BUDS

You will see in the photographs for this book that I love to experiment with different herbs and edible
flowers. I wish one day to be a better wild forager as it is always so surprising and exciting as a chef when
you discover that something that looks like a weed growing in the hedgerow is actually very good to eat.

As with all cooking, what you see in restaurants seems to change according to the latest trend. So a few
years ago it was nasturtiums, another year it was borage flowers and another wild meadowsweet. I have
been using dandelion leaves for many years, and then discovered that you can pickle the buds just like
capers, and the same goes for nasturtium, chive and chicory buds.

MAKES APPROX. 450G
50g dandelion buds
200ml rice wine vinegar
200ml water
1 garlic clove, smashed
1 tsp ground turmeric
1 tsp pink peppercorns

Place the dandelion buds in a 500ml sterilised, airtight jar (page 37).
Heat the remaining ingredients in a saucepan and gently simmer for
ten minutes to infuse the flavours. Allow to cool fully back to room
temperature and then pour over the buds.

Keep in the refrigerator for 6–8 weeks and then enjoy with fish, in
pasta dishes, salads and as garnishes.

PICKLED CARROTS

MAKES APPROX. 500G

250g organic carrots, washed
1 tsp grated fresh turmeric, or
    1 tsp ground
1 tsp grated fresh root ginger
1 garlic clove, crushed
1 tsp chilli paste or gochujang
    paste (a spicy Korean
    paste available in Asian
    supermarkets and some
    general supermarkets)
juice and zest of 1 lime
1 tbsp Pickled Mustard Seeds
    (page 40), optional
4 tbsp olive oil
1 tbsp cumin seeds
1 tbsp nigella seeds
12 curry leaves
300ml apple cider vinegar
1 tbsp coconut sugar

Chop the carrots into batons.

Mix together the turmeric, ginger, garlic, chilli or gochujang paste, lime juice, pickled mustard seeds, if using, and a little of the olive oil.

Heat the remaining olive oil in a saucepan and when hot add the cumin seeds, nigella seeds, lime zest and curry leaves. As the aromas are released, after about 30 seconds, add the carrots and the paste mix, stirring well in the pan.

Meanwhile, heat the apple cider vinegar in a separate pan and add the coconut sugar. When the sugar has dissolved, add the sweetened vinegar to the carrots, stir, and bring to the boil before reducing to a simmer for 10-15 minutes until the carrots are cooked but still with a bite.

Allow to cool and transfer to a sterilised, airtight jar (page 37). The pickle will keep for up to 2 weeks in the fridge.

GIARDINIERA

This is a recipe that reminds me of home. On picnics we would always have Tuna ftira sandwiches (page 158) with pickled vegetables – *giardiniera*. They are delicious at the start of a meal with some cheese or as a side to fish or chicken.

MAKES 1 LARGE JAR (APPROX. 1L)

1 small cauliflower, broken into florets
1 fennel bulb, sliced
6 baby carrots
2 celery sticks, halved lengthways and chopped into 2 inch batons
plenty of sea salt
3 tbsp extra virgin olive oil
1 or 2 bay leaves
500ml apple cider vinegar

Lay the vegetables in a shallow dish with plenty of salt, cover and leave overnight at room temperature.

The next day you will find some liquid has been released from the vegetables. Drain and rinse the vegetables well, then pat dry with kitchen paper and leave to dry over the next couple of hours before tossing in the extra virgin olive oil.

Pack the vegetables into a sterilised, airtight jar (page 37) along with the bay leaves.

Heat the apple cider vinegar in a pan until just boiling, take off the heat and pour into the jar until just covering the vegetables. Allow to cool before sealing.

Keep in a cool place – it will last for a month and continue to pickle during that time, so the vegetables will become increasingly sour on first bite!

KIMCHI

I go through phases where I can eat kimchi, a spicy fermented cabbage, with almost anything. Apparently it's pretty healthy, so maybe it balances out some of our less-healthy habits. I love that it adds a crunch and a hit of clean, spicy heat on the side – it's especially good with pork or smoked dishes.

MAKES APPROX. 500G

1 Chinese leaf cabbage
1 tbsp sea salt
25g Korean red pepper powder
50g Korean anchovy sauce
1 tbsp grated fresh root ginger
1 garlic clove, crushed
1 tbsp grated fresh turmeric
    root

Shred the Chinese leaf cabbage and separate out the leaves. Toss with the sea salt, making sure all the shredded leaves are evenly covered, then leave to sit for a couple of hours. Rinse and drain.

Mix together the Korean red pepper powder, Korean anchovy sauce and enough water to make a fairly runny paste. Mix this with the grated ginger, crushed garlic and grated turmeric, then mix all of this into the cabbage, massaging every leaf thoroughly with the paste.

Press the kimchi into a sterilised, airtight jar (page 37) so that a little liquid rises to the top to cover the cabbage. You need about 3cm of space between the liquid and the top of the jar, and it's important that the cabbage is submerged, so top up with a little water if needed.

Cover with the lid but don't fasten it, leave it loose, and keep at room temperature for a day to kickstart the fermentation process. After that, store in the fridge (keeping the lid loose) for up to a month.

PINK SAUERKRAUT

Sauerkraut is a milder relative of kimchi, again containing fermented cabbage, which provides a delicious sharp crunch on the side of lots of midweek dishes. It also happens to be really good for you. A happy discovery.

MAKES APPROX. 500G

1 white cabbage, shredded
    finely
50ml beetroot juice
sea salt

Place the shredded cabbage in a large bowl. Lightly sprinkle with salt and then knead the cabbage quite vigorously to release the natural juices before adding the beetroot juice and mixing everything together.

Pack the cabbage into a sterilised, airtight jar (page 37) and press down so that it is submerged in the liquid. You need about 3cm of space between the liquid and the top of the jar, and it's important that the cabbage is submerged, so top up with a little water if needed.

Seal the jar, but then remember to open it each day to release any built-up pressure. It will be ready after 3 days, but will continue to ferment and develop flavour beyond that time.

BABA GANOUSH

When friends come round for food I often make a bowl of aubergine baba ganoush, as it's so popular. It's slightly embarrassing when they ask for the recipe, as sometimes I don't use anything except the smoked aubergine and a little sea salt for seasoning. The classic recipe has tahini, but personally I prefer it without, as it has such an amazing flavour by itself. When I do decide to dress it up I'll go for classic Eastern Mediterranean flavours; I use a mix of seeds and ground spices, because while the spices infuse the flavour throughout the mix, I like the texture and intensity of the seeds. You can substitute grilled courgette, red pepper or baked sweet potato for the aubergine, if you like.

This is a great staple to have in the fridge during the week because it goes with so many dishes, or can be eaten as a dip, with cheese and crackers, on the side of a curry or with a salad.

MAKES APPROX. 200G

1 aubergine
1 tbsp extra virgin olive oil
sea salt, to finish

optional extras
1 Roast Garlic Confit (page 55), or regular, crushed
1 tbsp lemon juice
1 heaped tbsp Labneh (page 58) or Greek yoghurt

Using tongs to hold the aubergine, burn its skin directly over a medium-high gas hob flame, turning the aubergine every couple of minutes to make sure it is evenly scorched. If you don't have gas, the next best way is to use the grill on its highest setting, turning the aubergine every couple of minutes.

When the aubergine is burnt on all sides you will notice it almost deflates, which means it will be cooked and soft in the middle. Place it in a bowl, cover with cling film and leave to cool. This will enable the skin to peel off easily.

Once cool, peel and remove the clusters of seeds. On a chopping board, roughly smash them with a knife to a course texture. Mix in the olive oil and a good pinch of salt whilst still on the board using the knife. Add the garlic confit, lemon juice or labneh at the same time as the olive oil, if using. Then transfer to a bowl for serving.

AUBERGINE NAM PRIK

This is a type of relish or pickle that I love to have in the fridge on hand for adding to weekday dishes such as rice and Dhal (page 143), Chicken on the Rack (page 144), Pork in Whey (page 133), lamb or Sea Bream with Mung Kitchari (page 154). It's equally good with a piece of hard goat's cheese, some shredded baby gem lettuce and a slice of freshly baked sourdough.

MAKES APPROX. 500G

1 aubergine
50ml extra virgin olive oil
1/2 garlic clove
1 tsp tamarind paste
1 level tsp chilli flakes
1 tsp fish sauce
1 tsp palm or coconut sugar
1 tbsp finely chopped coriander
    leaves
1 tbsp finely chopped mint
    leaves
sea salt

Cut the aubergine into thick 4cm discs. Place in a large bowl with about a teaspoon of sea salt and a couple of tablespoons of the olive oil and rub the aubergine slices with this mix. Place the discs on a roasting tray and roast until a deep golden colour, about 20 minutes, turning halfway through. Allow the aubergine discs to cool a little, then cut into quarters.

Meanwhile, blitz the garlic, tamarind, chilli, fish sauce, sugar and remaining olive oil together in a food processor.

Combine this paste with the aubergine and chopped herbs. Transfer to a sterilised, airtight jar (page 37) and keep for up to 1 month in the fridge.

LOVAGE CHIMICHURRI

Lovage is a lesser-known herb (but one that grows as readily as parsley) which has a flavour with real punch. For me, it is a very good complement to white fish or chicken, ingredients that sometimes benefit from a lift. I have also used it in my Heritage Tomatoes with Lovage Chimichurri and Goat's Cheese (page 90). It's not something you can always easily find, but you can grow it in pots. I would also try substituting celery leaves if you can't find lovage.

MAKES APPROX. 500G JAR (including the oil)

50g picked and finely chopped lovage leaves (chopped weight)

50g picked flat-leaf parsley leaves and tender stems, coarsely chopped (about ½ large bunch)

50g picked coriander leaves and tender stems, coarsely chopped (about ½ large bunch)

50g chives, coarsely chopped

3 large garlic cloves, grated or crushed

2 tsp baby capers

1 tsp red chilli flakes

2 anchovies from a tin, drained and roughly chopped

2 tbsp sherry vinegar

100ml avocado oil

freshly ground black pepper

I prefer chopping all the herbs myself, and the most accurate way to do this is to first chop them one by one and then mix them all together with all the other ingredients in your jar – then you can easily shake this well before using each time. Leave in the fridge as part of your fridge larder but bring up to room temperature before using.

DEN MISO

This really simple recipe creates a paste that you can brush over so many things for instant flavour, especially when roasting aubergine (such as Baba Ganoush, page 51), or to be added to a pan of sautéed wild mushrooms or brushed over tofu or chicken before grilling.

MAKES APPROX. 200G

100g white miso paste
50g coconut sugar
30ml sake
30ml mirin

Mix all the ingredients together and heat in a pan for a few minutes. Leave to cool, then store in an airtight container in the fridge.

ROAST GARLIC CONFIT

This is a handy recipe, as the garlic keeps for up to a month and as you need them you can simply squeeze out the individual cloves.

5 whole garlic bulbs
250g rock salt

Place the garlic bulbs on some foil with the rock salt. Scrunch up the foil and seal, then roast at the oven's lowest temperature for 2–3 hours. Leave to cool, then store in an airtight container in the fridge.

FLAVOURED BUTTERS

I think the first flavoured butter I heard of back in Malta was 'Café de Paris' butter, which is flavoured with garlic, anchovies, Dijon mustard, capers, chives and parsley. When I had my restaurant in Malta I always wanted to try different things, some of which worked and others less so. I remember when I first served bone marrow we would literally give people the bone on a plate and they would just stare at it, not knowing what to do. Why am I talking about bone marrow? Because it is one of my favourite things on this planet and it is amazing in butter!

HOW TO MAKE A FLAVOURED BUTTER

Simply allow the butter to become soft enough so that you can beat in your flavour ingredients, then shape the butter into a log and chill it. Once it's cold, wrap it in cling film, knotting the ends, then you can unwrap and slice off discs as you need them. Flavoured butters will keep for a week in the fridge and about two months in the freezer.

NORI BUTTER

MAKES 125G

2 tbsp nori flakes
125g unsalted softened butter

Mix the nori flakes into the softened butter and follow the instructions above.

BONE MARROW BUTTER

MAKES APPROX. 275G

4–6 beef or veal marrow
  bones (available in some
  supermarkets and local
  butchers)
250g unsalted softened butter
½ tsp sea salt
½ tsp finely chopped fresh
  rosemary

Preheat the oven to 200°C, gas mark 6.

Place the marrow bones on a roasting tray, cut side up, and cook in the oven for about 15 minutes, until the marrow is soft. Allow to rest for a few minutes.

Scoop out the marrow using a long handled spoon and mix it with the butter, salt and rosemary, then follow the basic Flavoured Butter steps (see opposite).

WHIPPED SMOKED SALMON BUTTER

MAKES APPROX. 275G

50g unsalted butter, room
  temperature
2 tbsp whole milk
10g Hot Smoked Salmon
  (page 132), flaked

Add the butter and milk to a food processor and process on low setting until a whipped texture. Mix in the salmon flakes.

LABNEH AND WHEY

It is very pleasing to hang yoghurt. I see people's eyes rolling when I tell them to do this, but if you love meat you are going to understand why this is so useful, because it's actually the waste product from this process that is gold. The whey water you are left with makes the most amazing brining liquid, especially for cheaper cuts of meat that are full of flavour but sometimes aren't so tender. My favourite cuts to brine in whey, for anything from 24 hours up to 3 days, include Pork in Whey (page 133), Lamb Neck with Aubergine Nam Prik (page 130) and Onglet in Den Miso with Winter Slaw and Umeboshi Aioli (page 135). All you need is some muslin or cheesecloth, which you can buy online or from kitchen shops.

MAKES 1L

1 litre organic full-fat natural
   yoghurt

Line a sieve with the cloth and pour a tub of organic full-fat natural yoghurt into the centre. Pull up the corners of the cloth and tie them at the top – a rubber band is helpful for this. Place the sieve on top of a large mixing bowl and you'll notice the whey water beginning to strain through the cloth immediately. After a day you will have a thick yoghurt, or labneh, inside the cloth that makes wonderful simple dips – just add some lime zest, chopped preserved lemon or blitzed beetroot. Or the labneh can be spread on toast with honey or used as a cooling finish to any spicy dish. The traditional way to enjoy labneh is with za'atar and extra virgin olive oil on flatbread.

MAYO

I always think that when a recipe has to use only the egg whites, a quick mayo is a great way to use the yolks, and it's always a good thing to have in the fridge. The better the quality of the eggs, the more yellow, bright and flavoursome the mayo.

MAKES APPROX. 850G

3 egg yolks
juice of 1/2 lemon
1 tbsp Dijon mustard
1 tbsp apple cider vinegar
300ml vegetable oil

Place the egg yolks in a mixing bowl along with the lemon juice, mustard and vinegar and whisk it all together.

Slowly start to incorporate the vegetable oil. It is essential that you don't add the oil all in one go as this will cause the mayo to split. If it does split, slowly bring it back by adding a spoonful of lukewarm water. Keep in the fridge in an airtight jar for up to 2 weeks.

SOY CURED EGGS

MAKES 4

100ml soy sauce
25ml mirin
small strip of kombu
4 egg yolks

Mix together the soy sauce, mirin and kombu in a small bowl or sealable container. Gently place the egg yolks in the liquid, then cover tightly and leave to cure for about 6 hours. You can continue curing for up to 3 days and the yolks will harden to the point that you can grate them over pasta or rice dishes as an extra hit of umami.

SALT-CURED EGGS

MAKES 4

150g sea salt
100g coconut sugar or regular
    sugar
4 egg yolks

Combine the salt and sugar and add to a small, flat-bottomed sealable container. Make indentations and gently tip each yolk into its own indentation. Seal tightly and leave to cure for 3 days.

N.B. Both these recipes only use the egg yolks, but keep the whites when separating the eggs, and use for Consommé (page 27), Crab toast (page 29) or to make meringue.

BREAKFAST WITH FRIENDS

'"In the morning you will have the best food of your lives" said Achille.'

ANNIE PROULX, *BARKSKINS*

For me, breakfast has a thousand meanings. When working in a busy kitchen, breakfast is non-existent, except for vast amounts of coffee. But when we are off work, breakfast is a time of gratitude and nourishment. I love going out for breakfast – which in London has become a pastime that you could never tire of – just as much as cooking for friends and family, sharing and passing a few of the following dishes around the table. A good breakfast always leaves me feeling loved and positive about the rest of the day.

SCRAMBLED EGGS WITH COCONUT DUKKAH

For me, eggs are part of the essence of eating. Scrambled eggs are so easy and beautiful just with a scattering of salt. You need to go for it with the whisking, be generous with the butter and take off the heat before they are ready but keep stirring as they will then finish cooking in the residual heat. Then they will always be soft and the perfect breakfast.

SERVES 2

1 tbsp butter
4 free-range or organic eggs
1 tbsp crème fraîche or a splash
    of whole milk
sea salt
baby leaves, to serve

For the coconut dukkah
(makes 500g)
100g sesame seeds
250g hazelnuts, finely chopped
40g fennel seeds
40g coriander seeds
20g cumin seeds
50g dessicated coconut

First, make the Coconut Dukkah. Preheat the oven to 200°C / fan 180°C / gas mark 6. Mix all the ingredients in a bowl and then spread evenly on an oven tray. Roast in the oven for 2–3 minutes.

Remove from the oven and place the ingredients in a food processor. Pulse for a couple of seconds at a time to grind to a rough texture. This makes a large amount, so transfer to an airtight container and keep with your spices.

To make the eggs, heat a non-stick frying pan and add the butter. Meanwhile, crack the eggs into a mixing bowl and whisk vigorously. Add a generous pinch of salt and whisk in the crème fraîche or milk.

When the pan is nice and hot and the butter has melted, add the eggs. Using a spatula, move the eggs quickly in the pan to cook them through and keep them fluffy. When they are three-quarters cooked, take off the heat as they will finish cooking in the residual heat – this is called 'carry over cooking'.

Serve immediately in bowls and scatter over 1tbsp coconut dukkah and baby leaves. If you fancy, enjoy with a piece of sourdough toast and butter.

HOME-CURED BACON AND EGG

You might not believe the feeling of satisfaction you will get from making your own bacon. The process is relatively simple. First you need to brine a piece of pork belly for a few days, then smoke it over any flavoured tea of your preference. It should then be wrapped in cling film and either used as nice slices, as in this recipe, or chopped into chunks and used in anything from pasta to salads. Many people nowadays trim off the outside rind when cooking bacon, but I don't as the fat actually releases more flavour when sealing off the meat in a hot pan.

SERVES 6–8

For the bacon
150g coconut sugar
150g sea salt
1 tsp cumin seeds
1 tsp coriander seeds
1 tsp fennel seeds
600g pork belly
30g lemon and ginger loose tea leaves
150g rice (long or short grain)

For the egg
1 egg per person
sea salt and freshly ground black pepper
toast, to serve

Mix together the coconut sugar, salt and all the seeds. Place three-quarters of the mix in a sealable container and put the pork belly skin-side down into it. Scatter the remaining mix over the flesh. Seal the container and leave for 3 days in the fridge.

After that time, wash well under cold water and pat dry with kitchen paper.

In either your home smoker or a heatproof tray lined with foil, mix and scatter the tea and rice.

Heat the smoker or tray over a high heat on the hob until it starts to smoke, then lower the heat. On a rack which fits into the tray but is above the mixture, place the pork belly, skin-side down. Removing from the heat, put the lid on the smoker or cover very tightly with foil. Place back onto the hob, bring up to a high temperature again for 4–5 minutes, then lower to the lowest possible heat and leave for 2 hours. (It's a good idea to open a window!)

Take off the heat and let the meat rest in the smoking chamber/covered tray until cooled.

For anyone who remembers runny egg and soldiers as a child, this is my fondest earliest memory of food.

Boil the egg from cold water in a saucepan for 5 minutes, then drain and run it under a cold running tap. Once cool enough to touch, peel and mash the egg, season, then spread on toast and serve with 2 slivers of fried bacon.

POACHED EGGS WITH ELDERFLOWER HOLLANDAISE

Poached eggs have a way of mirroring your mood. The perfect poached egg on a weekend morning is the pinnacle of happiness.

Having to prep 400 poached eggs every Saturday morning was one of the bittersweet memories I have of life as a commis chef. My number one piece of advice is to find the deepest pot you can find as the egg needs to 'drop' into the water. Let the water boil, then lower a touch, add your vinegar and drop the egg into simmering water, while listening to Jack Johnson.

SERVES 2

150g unsalted butter
4 free-range or organic eggs
    (the fresher the better)
3 tsp elderflower vinegar
    (shop-bought or see page
    39)
1 tbsp white wine vinegar
200g spring greens, shredded
1 English muffin, cut in half and
    toasted
sea salt and freshly ground
    black pepper

For the Hollandaise, melt 125g of the butter and skim away any white solids. Keep the butter warm while you bring a pan of water to a simmer and then, in a bowl that fits over the top of the pan, whisk together 2 egg yolks and 3 teaspoons of elderflower vinegar until you have an airy foam (sabayon). Remove this from the heat and whisk in a little of the butter before putting it back over the heat, whisking all the time. Repeat until all the butter is added and you have a mayonnaise texture. Season with sea salt and freshly ground black pepper to taste.

To poach the 2 eggs, bring a saucepan of water to the boil, add a splash of white wine vinegar and reduce to a simmer. Stir the water a little to create a whirlpool, then crack each egg into a cup and slide gently into the water, one at a time. Leave to poach for 3–4 minutes, depending on how soft you like your egg. Remove with a slotted spoon.

Sauté the shredded spring greens in a frying pan in a little butter to soften, and season.

Place the toasted muffin halves on two plates then divide the spring greens between the two and top with the poached eggs. Pour over some elderflower Hollandaise and serve.

OMELETTES

While working at The Modern Pantry I was won over to Anna Hansen's way of life and cooking through one particular simple technique: how she would make an omelette. It was all about the heat of the pan, so that the egg mixture would hit that heat and immediately puff up, forming the softest, fluffiest omelette which she would then finish either simply with picked coriander and sliced spring onion garnish or turn into a feast with sambal prawns.

At home I will make an omelette with whatever we have, and the fridge larder always comes in handy here. I might serve an omelette with a spoonful of Baba Ganoush (page 51) and some baby kale leaves, or some yoghurt and a spoonful of Lovage Chimichurri (page 54). I like to sauté wild mushrooms, then deglaze the pan with a little balsamic vinegar and add these juices to the omelette just before flipping.

SERVES 1

2 large free-range or organic
   eggs (the fresher the better)
1/2 tbsp butter
1/2 tbsp vegetable oil
sea salt

Heat a medium frying pan over a high heat. Beat the eggs with a balloon whisk and season with a generous pinch of salt.

When the pan is very hot, add the butter and oil and, once it is bubbling hot, throw in your omelette mixture. You are hoping for a Yorkshire pudding-style effect as the edges should immediately puff up. Don't be tempted to lift the pan and move the raw egg from the centre of the pan to the edges. Keep it flat on the heat and wait until you have a 5cm circle of still-runny egg in the middle (depending on the eggs, this will take 2–4 minutes). Flip the omelette into a half moon and immediately slide onto the warm plate.

FRENCH TOAST WITH CLOVE SUGAR AND CARDAMOM COMPOTE

We went to stay with our friend Emma and her daughter Violet in the South of France and my present to Violet was teaching her how to make French toast. This is a sweet toast, so I've used 'clove' sugar here, but you can use any flavoured sugars. I love star anise, lavender and vanilla.

This recipe will make enough compote that you will have some leftover to serve with yoghurt, granola or porridge. Store it in an airtight, sterilised jar (page 37) and it will keep in the fridge for a week.

SERVES 4 TO SHARE

2 eggs
100ml whole milk
olive oil, for frying
4 slices brioche
1/2 tbsp butter
2 tsp clove sugar (2 tsp sugar
    mixed with 1/4 tsp ground
    cloves)

For the cardamom compote
250g mixed berries (frozen is
    good for this recipe)
50g coconut syrup or agave
    syrup
seeds from 8 cardamom pods

First make the compote. Simply put the fruit, syrup, cardamom seeds and a little water in a pan and heat gently for about 15 minutes until reduced to a compote consistency. You may need to add more water as you go.

For the French toast, preheat the oven to 180°C / fan 160°C / gas mark 4. Whisk the eggs and milk together in a large mixing bowl.

Heat a large non-stick, ovenproof frying pan and when very hot add a small drizzle of olive oil. Dip the brioche slices one by one into the egg mixture and then place in the pan. Leave for a few minutes (don't be tempted to move them about) so they can get a nice golden colour, then flip them onto the other side until golden. Add a knob of butter to the pan and place in the oven for 2–3 minutes to puff the toast.

Serve the toast along with some compote and sprinkled with clove sugar.

SMOKED AND GRILLED MACKEREL WITH CELERIAC REMOULADE ON AN ENGLISH MUFFIN

I have included a chapter on smoking, brining and curing at home (page 121–137) in this book and I'd really recommend giving it a go for this recipe. Smoking the mackerel before you grill it will help to crisp up the skin and release even more flavour through those precious oils. Of course, you can buy very good smoked mackerel from fishmongers, but I just love how it is possible to do this ourselves on the hob with a small steel box (bought online), adding different flavours to the smoke with the myriad teas that seem to appear from nowhere in our cupboards.

SERVES 2

For smoking the mackerel
50g jasmine rice
50g oolong tea
2 mackerel fillets

For the celeriac remoulade
1 small celeriac, peeled
1 tsp horseradish
2 tsp wholegrain mustard
1 tsp Mayo (page 58)
sea salt
lemon juice, plus extra to serve

1 English muffin
butter, for spreading

To smoke the mackerel, line the bottom of the smoking tray or a heatproof tray with foil and scatter over the rice and tea.

Set the rack over the mixture, sitting just above it. Light the hob and place the smoker over the heat. Let the aroma begin to fill the room (best to open a window!).

Place the 2 mackerel fillets on the rack and lower the heat. Put the lid on the smoker or cover the tray very tightly with foil and let it smoke slowly on a low heat for 5 minutes.

Take off the heat and let the mackerel rest in the smoking chamber for another hour or so.

For the celeriac remoulade, cut the celeriac into equal-sized thin julienne slices, making sure you have a firm base to start with to prevent the celeriac from rolling, making it dangerous.

In a mixing bowl, combine the horseradish, mustard and mayo. Taste to check you like the balance and adjust as needed. Add the celeriac and mix well to coat. Season and add lemon juice to taste.

When the mackerel is smoked, place it under the grill, skin-side up, for 5 minutes until the skin is crispy. Meanwhile, split and toast the muffin, spread with butter and add some celeriac remoulade. Top with the mackerel and serve, squeezing over more fresh lemon juice.

PICKLED PEACHES WITH GOAT'S CURD ON SOURDOUGH

This recipe reminds me of Malta, where peaches ripen in the summer heat and the raw goat's cheese from the neighbouring island of Gozo is so fresh and mild and is perfect with grilled peaches. Goat's curd is softer and milder than goat's cheese and you can find it in some supermarkets, delis and cheese shops. Clover flowers pop up all over the place, although like any foraging you just need to be sure they are clean before you use them.

SERVES 4 TO SHARE

2 ripe peaches
60ml apple cider vinegar
1 tsp sugar
2 slices sourdough
2 tbsp Rosemary-infused Oil
    (page 38) or extra virgin olive
    oil
50ml white balsamic vinegar
5g sugar
2 tbsp goat's curd (or
    mascarpone)
sea salt
clover flowers, to serve
    (optional)

To pickle the peaches, cut them in half, remove the stones, slice the flesh and toss with the vinegar, sugar and a good pinch of sea salt. Let sit for 10 minutes

Meanwhile, heat a griddle pan, brush the sourdough on both sides with the oil and when the pan is very hot, griddle the toast. Put the toast in a very low oven to keep warm while you prepare the rest of the dish.

Use the same pan to griddle the peaches until hot and scorched. Don't move them too much, as you want to keep those sharp grill lines. Pop these in the oven along with the toast.

To make the balsamic reduction, add the vinegar and sugar to a small frying pan and heat, stirring continuously until you have a syrup consistency.

To serve, arrange the peach slices on the toast and top with small spoonfuls of goat's curd. Drizzle over the balsamic reduction and scatter over the herbs and flowers. Your friends will love you forever.

KOJI RICE RAMEN WITH CURED EGG

I wanted to include koji rice as an ingredient, even though I'm very aware of how difficult it can be to source unusual ingredients. But koji rice is fascinating because it is so fundamental to many of the Japanese ingredients we now have in our cupboards, including miso, soy sauce, mirin and sake. Fortunately it is now found quite easily online.

Similar to sourdough starter, Koji rice is used as a starter in Japanese cooking to make such common ingredients as miso, mirin, sake and soy sauce. It is cooked rice that has been inoculated with a mould called aspergillus oryzae. Just as sauerkraut is fermented cabbage, koji rice is essentially fermented or mouldy rice and is often the base of that 'umami' or sweet savoury taste associated with lots of Japanese dishes. For example miso is made by mixing cooked soybeans, water and salt with koji rice.

This breakfast dish started out as an idea because on Buddhist retreats after waking up at 5am to meditate till 8, most days my mind would be thinking of how hungry I was and however much I wanted to let thoughts wash in and out, the hot bowl of ramen rice handed to me at 8.05 was what I would mostly focus on. This breakfast bowl has a special place in my heart in which I remember how easy it is to simply obsess on a bowl of hot rice for breakfast.

This recipe works very well without the addition of the koji rice, it simply adds to that amazing umami flavour. I have also used it to tenderise steak (page 136) where it has a similar, if not better, effect to very expensive dry ageing.

SERVES 2

100g short grain rice
30g koji mould, crumbled
5g unsalted butter
125ml sake
125ml light soy sauce
125ml mirin
1 tsp ginger, grated
2 baby carrots
2 asparagus tips
1 Salt-cured Egg (page 61)

Wash the rice under cold water. Add to a saucepan, cover with water and bring to the boil. Reduce to a low simmer and add your crumbled koji

Let simmer for 20 minutes, stirring gently and often throughout. When the rice is cooked, drain, then return to the pot, add butter and let rest while you make the ramen sauce.

Combine the sake, soy sauce, mirin and ginger in a small saucepan and bring to a low simmer. Remove the pan from the heat and allow to infuse for 10 minutes.

Slice the carrots and asparagus very thinly.

Now bring all the elements together in one pan, heating through gently. Serve in bowls with a cured egg.

ALL I EAT IS LETTUCE

The title for this chapter came from taking one of my British friends to Malta. She is vegan, which was an opportunity to test both the culinary skills of a number of Maltese chefs and her sense of humour. One chef shrugged his shoulders when I noticed chicken stock in the potatoes and pointed out that wasn't exactly vegan, 'Mela, she is a rabbit' was his response.

I actually really enjoyed stripping back my own cooking biases to create dishes for my friend. And after working at Yotam Ottolenghi's restaurant, Nopi, I had even more appreciation for how vegetables and salads can be the main event of a meal.

I've been asked to cater for a number of weekend workshops and a yoga supper club where the salads always get people talking as, again, thanks to Nopi and my own love of presenting food I will bring out platters of wild combinations that give big bursts of flavour. I was even talked into doing a few salads for my own wedding; I'll never forget standing in the kitchen in my wedding dress trying not to get saffron yoghurt on myself as I dressed the aubergine!

EDIBLE FLOWERS

A friend of mine who is an acupuncturist taught me that flowers nourish our heart energy, and I think that discovering edible flowers is one of my most favourite things. This list isn't exhaustive, but I've included some favourites:

Anise hyssop
The flowers and the leaves are edible and have a delicious anise flavour (see page 24 for my Chicken Stock Risotto with Anise Hyssop and Baby Kale Tempura)

Apple blossom
These are so beautiful and sweet tasting as a garnish for desserts

Basil blossom
Delicious in cocktails or to garnish a pasta dish

Borage flowers
These are so pretty, especially in tomato salads. The leaves are quite prickly though so just enjoy the flowers

Chamomile flowers
Usually used to make a calming tea, I do like to scatter some dried chamomile flower tea at the bottom of the tray when roasting sweet potatoes, adding a little water to release the flavour

Chive flowers
Chives grow so easily and sometimes I'll make a simple dressing of crème fraîche and chopped chives with a little sake (Japanese wine), toss in some roasted cauliflower florets and scatter over the chive flowers

Citrus blossom
I love using orange blossom water and the flowers are equally as flavourful, just a few petals go a long way. Labneh (page 58) or yoghurt is delicious with a few petals scattered over

Clover flowers
It's funny I have seen lawns of clover with bees rushing from flower to flower and only recently discovered that these flowers are indeed edible for us too and are lovely and sweet. They were the perfect garnish for the Pickled Peaches with Goat's Curd on Sourdough (page 77) which I also drizzled with a little honey

Courgette, squash and pumpkin flowers
Stuffed courgette flowers are well known, but I didn't realise you could do the same with squash and pumpkin

Elderflower
I will never forget having elderflower tempura on the best dessert I've ever eaten at Spring by Skye Gyngell. It was a very delicate, citrus based tart. It was incredible

Fennel fronds
These grow wild everywhere in Malta and are so pretty. They have a lovely mild aniseed flavour

French marigolds
These are such an amazing orange colour, they really add drama to a salad

Meadowsweet
Perhaps more the domain of the botanical cocktail maker but this common wildflower is becoming more popular with chefs, especially the buds that have a marzipan flavour

Nasturtiums
Still one of my favourites as both the leaves and the flowers are delicious

Pansies
These are again very pretty, especially for decorating cakes

Radish flowers
The spicy, peppery taste of radishes is the perfect way to add a little heat and fire to a cool summer salad and the flowers, being milder in taste, are a beautiful echo of that flavour

Roses
A good friend told me that flowers are good for the heart and none more so than rose. The petals are most often used to decorate cakes, but the flavour also goes well with Middle Eastern dishes – think of rose harissa – and they are a very romantic addition to a gin cocktail

Runner bean flowers
The flowers of peas and beans perhaps unsurprisingly taste like a milder version of the pea or bean itself

Sea kale
I am a bit obsessed with seaweed and sea 'plants' such as samphire and sea kale. With sea kale you can also eat the flowers, which have a nutty flavour and so are delicious with fish

Violets
Fortunately violets are something I can grow in my window boxes - they have such delicate blooms

Wild garlic flowers
During the spring if you are driving or walking in the British countryside you will know that certain smell of the wild garlic growing. When in flower, it produces an amazing carpet of delicate white flowers on the woodland floor. A simple pasta dish of orzo, extra virgin olive oil, wilted wild garlic, shavings of Parmigiano Reggiano and wild garlic flowers makes me very happy

CARROT SALAD WITH FRIENDS

The importance of a good big mixing bowl is the best lesson in making salads that you need to learn. This allows you to toss well, build flavour, stack tall and create height as you plate the perfect salad. This recipe takes the humble carrot and puts it on a pedestal, through three ways of preparing it. All that effort is definitely worth it, but I would say to save it for when you have quite a few good friends around to impress.

SERVES 8

juice of 2 limes and 1 orange
   (see brined carrots below)
handful of chives, roughly
   chopped, plus 8 chive
   flowers, if you have them
good-quality extra virgin olive
   oil, for drizzling

For the brined carrots
2 bay leaves
5 black peppercorns
250ml rice vinegar
50g sugar
pinch of crushed red pepper
   flakes
50g sea salt
500g baby carrots
1 tbsp olive oil

For the carrots in sake and butter
4 carrots
1 tbsp coconut oil
250ml sake
50g butter

For the roasted baby carrots
200g baby heritage carrots
   (mixed colours)
zest of 2 limes and 1 orange
2 tbsp olive oil
1/2 tsp sea salt

For the brined carrots, bring the bay leaves, peppercorns, vinegar, sugar, red pepper flakes and salt to the boil in a large saucepan. Pour the brining liquid over the baby carrots in a heatproof bowl and allow to cool. Remove the carrots and pat dry with kitchen paper. (Save the brine to pickle another batch of vegetables.)

Preheat the grill to medium-high. Toss the brined baby carrots with the oil in a large bowl and season lightly with salt. Grill, turning occasionally, until lightly charred in spots.

For the carrots in sake and butter, cut the carrots in circles on a slant. Heat the coconut oil in a hot pan, then add the carrots. Cook, tossing occasionally, until caramelised. Deglaze the pan with the sake, then add the butter and take off the heat to let them rest.

For the roasted baby heritage carrots, preheat the oven to 220°C/ fan 200°C/, gas mark 7. In a bowl, toss the carrots in the lime and orange zest, olive oil and salt. Roast in the oven for 30 minutes until golden.

To assemble the salad, add all the carrots to a large mixing bowl. Squeeze over the juice of the limes and orange. Add the chopped chives to the bowl along with the chive flowers, if you have them. Drizzle over a couple of tablespoons of extra virgin olive oil and gently toss all the elements of the salad together. Taste to see if you would like to add extra salt. Pile onto a serving platter and place in the centre of the table.

HERITAGE TOMATOES WITH LOVAGE CHIMICHURRI AND GOAT'S CHEESE

The Lovage Chimichurri dressing for this salad (page 54) complements the sweetness of the tomatoes. I specify Maltese goat's cheese here but of course you could experiment with any goat's or sheep's cheese. Cheese and tomato will always be a perfect match. As in Italy, basil is the favoured herb in Malta for a tomato salad, but I have loved discovering so many different herbs while in the UK, and especially all the varieties of mint. I live close to Petersham Nurseries in London and it's there that I discovered apple, chocolate, grapefruit and orange mints. And you don't need very green fingers, as they are so easy to grow.

SERVES 4

500g mixed heritage tomatoes,
   sliced at the last minute
100g Maltese peppered goat's
   cheese, crumbled
2 tbsp Lovage Chimichurri
   (page 54)
2 tbsp extra virgin olive oil
sea salt and freshly ground
   black pepper
apple mint, to garnish

Arrange the tomato slices on a serving dish and crumble over the goat's cheese. Drizzle over the lovage chimichurri and olive oil. Scatter over a good pinch of salt, black pepper and apple mint leaves.

BELUGA LENTILS WITH ASPARAGUS

This is a hearty salad with lots of bite. Beluga lentils aren't as popular as Puy and you can use either, but I love the texture of beluga lentils, being slightly softer than Puy.

SERVES 4 AS A SIDE
(or 2 as a main)

200g beluga lentils, rinsed

400ml vegetable stock or
   water

100g giant couscous

1 bunch of asparagus

4 tbsp olive oil

sea salt

1 tsp crushed red pepper flakes

1/2 tsp cumin seeds

1 bunch of coriander (25g),
   chopped

1 bunch of parsley (25g),
   chopped

1 garlic clove, crushed

juice of 1/2 lemon

1 chicory bulb, separated into
   leaves

2 slices sourdough, roughly cut
   into crouton-size pieces

Place the lentils in a saucepan and cover with stock or water, then bring to the boil, lower to a simmer and cook for about 25 minutes until the lentils are cooked but not mushy.

In another saucepan, cover the giant couscous with water, bring to the boil and reduce to a simmer until cooked – check the packet instructions, but this should be about 10 minutes. Drain any residual liquid and keep covered with a tea towel.

Snap off the woody ends of the asparagus and cut on the diagonal into thirds. Mix with 1 tablespoon of the olive oil, the red pepper flakes and cumin seeds, season with salt and toss in a hot frying pan for about 5 minutes. Set aside.

Using the same pan, heat the remaining oil and fry the sourdough croutons until crisp. Drain on kitchen paper.

To make the dressing, combine the chopped herbs with the remaining olive oil, crushed garlic, lemon juice and a little salt.

Now you can build your salad. Mix the lentils and couscous together and place onto the plate. Add the asparagus, chicory leaves and croutons. To serve, pour over the dressing.

AUBERGINE, EDAMAME AND CUCUMBER SALAD

If I'm honest, I always feel that every aubergine recipe is an adaptation of something from Nopi, but this is a perfect example of a blank canvas. The cutting of the aubergine into huge discs, tossing with the energy from all your body in vast amounts of olive oil and salt and then roasting in a searing hot oven until you get perfect brown colouring. That is what I learnt from Nopi; whatever dressing, crunch and garnish you give a dish is your take or masterpiece to call your own.

SERVES 6

3 aubergine, sliced into thick
    3cm discs
olive oil, for drizzling
3 tbsp Den Miso (page 55)
100g edamame beans
extra virgin olive oil, for
    drizzling
1 tsp grated turmeric (or ground)
2 tbsp lemon juice
200g Greek yoghurt
sea salt and freshly ground
    black pepper
1 small Lebanese cucumber,
    sliced with a peeler into
    ribbons
handful of coriander
Pickled Mustard Seeds (page 40)

Preheat the oven to 220°C / fan 200°C / gas mark 7.

Toss the aubergine slices in plenty of olive oil and salt. Place in the oven, spread out on a baking tray and roast for about 20 minutes, turning halfway through, until a deep golden colour and soft in the middle.

Meanwhile, heat a frying pan and toss the edamame beans in the den miso for 2-3 minutes. Set aside.

Combine the turmeric, lemon juice and yoghurt. With a slotted spoon, 'splatter' the turmeric yoghurt dressing over the aubergine slices.

Scatter over the edamame beans, then garnish with cucumber ribbons, coriander and Pickled Mustard Seeds.

TEMPURA TOFU WITH TURMERIC

With turmeric being added to all we eat as a natural ingredient that fights most illnesses, and tofu having no character or flavour at all, the joining of dots for me was an instant one. What if we pressed tofu in turmeric water for a few days? You'll need to prepare the tofu the night before serving (at least) – or you can add it to the tempura flour. If you don't have galangal you can substitute with ginger.

SERVES 4

1 tsp grated turmeric
1/2 tsp grated galangal
1 tbsp tamarind paste
1 tbsp honey, or to taste
400g tofu, cut into bite-sized
   pieces
100g tempura flour
500ml sunflower oil
Chinese wilted greens and
   homemade chilli and soy
   sauce, to serve

Boil the turmeric, galangal (or ginger) in water for about 30 minutes, until it becomes slightly creamy; add more water if the concoction starts looking a bit dry.

Add the tamarind and honey, whisk and add the tofu. Transfer to a dish, cover with cling film and place something heavy on top of the tofu – this helps to submerge the tofu properly in the liquid. Place in the fridge and leave to infuse overnight. Remove the tofu pieces from the liquid and pat dry with paper towels and then coat in tempura flour.

In a wok, heat the oil up to 180°C (test either with a kitchen thermometer, or using a little bit of tempura flour – it is ready if it crisps quickly when you drop it in). Fry the tofu pieces one by one, making sure you lower the heat when the oil starts to get too hot, until the tempura is puffed up and browning. Use tongs to turn the tofu pieces over to ensure they become golden on all sides. Remove with a slotted spoon and drain on paper towels.

Serve with home-made chilli and soy sauce on some Chinese wilted greens.

RAW AND WHOLE

Two of my favourite food principles are at play here: creating dishes from raw ingredients and whole ingredients. Food can be served to comfort, to make people smile and hopefully get the conversation going, too. When I want to get everyone talking I find the easiest way is by presenting raw ingredients that really awaken people's tastebuds at the beginning of a meal. I realise not everyone wishes to try all my combinations but they are always an ice breaker.

Another favourite food ethos of mine is to cook an ingredient 'whole'. I have taken to roasting vegetables this way after eating whole roasted celeriac at a restaurant called Roberta's in Brooklyn. It reminds me of those old traditions of baking vegetables in the embers of the fire, and in some cultures, cooking meat underground in a fire pit. These ways of cooking feel primal and in complete honour of the ingredients.

OYSTERS WITH KIMCHI WATER

I find oysters are always fun to start a celebration – it gets people laughing. There are so many ways and condiments with which to serve them, including bourbon. But since we love it when they come with tabasco, I decided to try using the liquid that comes out of kimchi. I think this was during my phase of adding kimchi to every dish I cooked or ate.

SERVES 4

8 oysters
30ml kimchi water (page 48)

It isn't easy to describe how to shuck an oyster, and if you aren't sure how my first recommendation would be to ask at an oyster bar for a quick demonstration as it is quite simple when you know how.

I start by holding the oyster at the round end with a tea towel and feeling for a tiny gap in the shell with an oyster shucker or small knife. You get a feel for knowing just where the oyster shell is willing to give and come apart. Once you find that small hole, wiggle around it, levering the top of the shell off. With the shell off, use the knife to disconnect the bottom of the oyster from the shell (it is connected with a 'valve') and check for any bits of shell before serving.

Serve on ice in the centre of the table with a small dipping bowl of kimchi water and a couple of small spoons to drizzle the water onto the oyster.

SEA BASS CARPACCIO

As a chef, I am very romantic about fish, especially when I know it is very fresh. I might take a fillet and very lightly grill it and as soon as it comes out of the oven I will just flake it and eat it with my fingers, or in this case take an incredibly fresh raw fillet and just slice very thinly, squeeze over lemon and salt and make a fuss with a few fresh and pickled radishes and a little mirin dressing. This is the kind of dish to try when you know you have a just-caught fish.

SERVES 2 (as a sharing plate)

1 sea bass fillet, skin on
squeeze of lemon juice
3 Pickled Radishes (page 43)
2 fresh radishes
a few young nasturtium leaves,
    optional
sea salt

For the dressing
50ml Rosemary-infused Oil
    (page 38)
1 tbsp mirin
1 tbsp honey

Place the fillet skin-side down on your board. Check the fillet has no bones remaining; use kitchen tweezers to remove any you find.

Slowly from the tail end, cut thin slices horizontally through the flesh. You will get a feel for how to go with the flesh.

Arrange the slices horizontally on the plate, squeeze over some lemon juice and season with salt.

Add the pickled and fresh radishes to your plate, alternating pickled and raw. Garnish with young nasturtium leaves, if you have them.

Whisk the three elements of the dressing together – do not worry if it splits, as it will come together again easily. Drizzle the dressing lightly back and forth, up and down a few times onto your perfect plated carpaccio.

TUNA BELLY WITH TIGER'S MILK

Forgive me, for this recipe is not exactly 'everyday' but I wanted to show the inner workings of a chef's mind. I had to find a specialist fishmonger for the prized tuna belly and one small piece cost a breathtaking amount, but once I tasted it I knew why this would be considered so highly as a sushi ingredient. It's incredibly rich and so it turns out you would only need a little for it to go a long way. Like many delicacies today, the belly of the tuna used to be thrown away but as tastes for oily fish have grown, the appeal of this part of the fish has increased. As tuna belly is rich, it's not to everyone's taste, so this recipe would work equally well with regular tuna from your fishmonger or supermarket, seared just on the outside and left rare in the middle

Tiger's milk is the Peruvian term for the citrus marinade that is used to cure seafood in ceviche dishes. In Peru it is sometimes served along with the ceviche in a shot glass, and so I decided to try serving the tuna belly in a little tiger's milk. The citrus cuts through the richness of the tuna belly perfectly.

SERVES 2–4 (sharing plate)

100g tuna belly
sea salt
handful of nasturtium leaves
1 tbsp Pickled Mustard Seeds
　　(page 40)

For the tiger's milk
1 small red onion, sliced
1 chilli, deseeded and sliced
small bunch of coriander,
　　bashed with a rolling pin
50ml milk
juice of 1 lime

Place all the tiger's milk ingredients in a kilner jar with a lid and store overnight in the fridge.

When ready to use, shake well and strain through a muslin cloth.

Pour some of the tiger's milk into a flat or shallow bowl.

Slice the tuna belly, season and arrange in the bowl. Add the nasturtium leaves and pickled mustard seeds and serve.

LAMB TARTARE

This dish was mentioned in passing one day by Hyunggyu Kim during my time at the Corinthia Hotel in London, when he was the executive sous chef. It was a refreshing inspiration at a time of immense hard work and anything he said seemed to register with me, to then be used years later.

The importance of this dish is in the quality of the lamb, so it is sensible to build a relationship with your butcher so that you can ask for a piece of fresh lamb loin that you wish to use for a tartare. The result is a plate of such flavour and freshness. For me, this is the appreciation of meat.

SERVES 4 (as an appetiser)

1 banana shallot, chopped to a
   fine brunoise (page 14)
1 celery stick, chopped to a
   brunoise
1 tsp freshly grated horseradish
1 tbsp soy sauce
1 tbsp Worcestershire sauce
1 tsp sugar
½ tsp mustard powder
250g lamb loin
2 spring onions, finely sliced
1 quail's egg

Mix all the ingredients together apart from the lamb, spring onions and quail's egg and leave in the fridge overnight.

When ready to make the dish, finely dice the lamb loin, cutting away and discarding any fat. Allow to come to room temperature.

In a mixing bowl, combine the lamb with the dressing and toss a few times.

Serve in the middle of a nice plate, garnishing with the spring onions. Crack a quail's egg very gently and, swapping the yolk from each half of the shell to the other, separate it from the white. This requires great patience. Serve the yolk in one of the halves of the shell in the centre of your tartare.

RIB-EYE TATAKI WITH SOY SESAME DRESSING AND TOASTED RICE

Tataki means either raw or lightly seared, but I recommend very lightly searing the steak for this recipe. This might normally be made with a less fatty cut of meat, such as fillet steak, however, I am a bit obsessed with rib-eye and the flavour here is incredible, which all comes from the marbling of the fat through the flesh.

The dish came about when I was working as a private chef in Ibiza. I ended up on a boat being asked to make canapés with just a handful of ingredients. I had some rib-eye, some tamari sauce, sesame oil and limes. Funnily enough, they wanted more than I could make, which shows cooking is so often about making the best dish from what you have.

SERVES 4 (as an appetiser)

300g rib-eye steak
Mustard-infused Oil (page 38)
 or sesame oil
sea salt and freshly ground
 black pepper
spring onion, julienned
toasted rice, to garnish

Soy sesame dressing
25ml tamari sauce
25ml sesame oil
zest and juice of 1 lime
½ tsp finely julienned pickled
 ginger
pinch of nori flakes

Trim the fatty 'eye' end off the rib-eye steak. Keep this for adding to a beef stir-fry.

Rub the steak with oil, season and in a really hot pan sear (see Glossary, page 14) very quickly and equally on each side. Take out of the pan and rest. When cool, wrap in cling film very tightly and rest in the fridge for up to 2 days.

When ready to serve, cut thinly with a sharp knife, arrange the slices on the plate and drizzle with mustard oil . Bring up to room temperature.

Mix all the dressing ingredients together, then drizzle over the meat and garnish with fresh spring onions and toasted rice.

WHOLE ROASTED CAULIFLOWER

This has become one of my favourite dishes as it is so simple, beautiful and creates a sweetness that we love. I started to roast cauliflowers whole at the school, so we roast three big trays of them in one go. The children love to see them whole with their leaves still on before breaking them up and serving them to each other.

SERVES 4

1 cauliflower
4–5 tbsp olive oil
plenty of sea salt
2–3 tbsp natural yoghurt
3 spring onions, thinly sliced
2 tbsp toasted mixed seeds
    (hemp, sunflower, sesame
    flax or pumpkin)

Preheat the oven to 220°C / fan 200°C / gas mark 7.

All you do is put the cauliflower in a casserole pot, drizzle with plenty of olive oil and scatter over some sea salt.

Cover and roast in the oven for 10 minutes until soft and coloured, then lower the heat to 190°C / fan 170°C / gas mark 5 for another 40 minutes–1 hour. The exact time will depend on the size and freshness of the cauliflower, but you want to be able to pierce it easily with a sharp knife.

I then allow it to rest a little before serving, keeping it whole for the presentation. I spoon over some natural yoghurt, thinly sliced spring onion and throw over plenty of toasted seeds for crunch to contrast with the softness of the cauliflower. After we have had our fill, it makes the base for a perfect salad for the next day with some cooked grains and fresh leaves.

POINTED CABBAGE WITH ORANGE TAMARIND DRESSING AND A SIDE OF PARTRIDGE

In this recipe the main event is the roasted cabbage. I remember a meal at Blue Hill Restaurant, in New York City, where one of the courses was a carrot. It was treated with as much reverence as a sirloin steak and since then I have always done my best to think about the flavour and presentation of vegetables equally, perhaps even more so than for meat or fish. And so in this recipe the cabbage takes centre stage, with a side of roast partridge that goes beautifully with the flavours of the orange tamarind dressing.

SERVES 2

For the roasted cabbage
1/2 pointed cabbage
olive oil, for brushing
sea salt

For the orange tamarind dressing
zest and juice of 2 oranges
2 Roast Garlic Confit cloves (see page 55), or crushed garlic
3 tbsp extra virgin olive oil
1 tbsp apple cider vinegar
2 tbsp tamarind paste

For the partridge
1 partridge
250ml chicken or vegetable stock
2 tbsp vegetable oil
a small handful of thyme sprigs
sea salt

To serve
50ml seasoned buttermilk (optional)

Preheat the oven to 200°C /fan 180°C / gas mark 6.

Brush the cut side of the cabbage with olive oil and season with sea salt.

Put into a roasting tin and cook in the oven for about 25 minutes, then reduce the temperature to 160°C/140°C fan oven/gas mark 3 and continue to roast for 10-15 minutes, until the edges become golden and the cabbage is tender.

While the cabbage is roasting, put the orange zest and juice into a mixing bowl. Whisk in the other dressing ingredients until fully combined and set aside.

Then prepare the partridge. First, poach the bird by placing it into a saucepan with the chicken or vegetable stock, bring it to a gentle simmer and poach for 3 minutes. Remove from the liquid, set aside and season all over.

Heat the oil in a frying pan. When hot, place the partridge into the pan, breast side down, and throw in the thyme. Evenly pan roast the bird by turning it frequently and basting with the hot oil. When nicely golden, remove and allow to rest for at least 5 minutes.

To serve, pour the dressing over the cabbage, allowing it to fill the serving plate and to be used to dip the partridge in. If you like you can also serve a small sauce bowl of seasoned buttermilk to drizzle over everything.

HAY-ROASTED PURPLE POTATOES

The idea for this dish came from a childhood memory of piercing potatoes with a fork, covering them in foil and putting them in the bbq while the day became evening at the beach during the summer. Then as I began to cook for myself I would make jacket potatoes almost every evening with every filling combination you can imagine. Sweet potatoes then crept into the equation, followed by purple potatoes. And then as I began to read about and taste foods cooked in hay I thought, why not give potatoes a try? It turns out they took on a lovely flavour. I decided to add some chamomile because I had tried a recipe for roasting sweet potatoes in chamomile tea and that had been delicious too.

So this recipe is a direct look into the mind of a chef, putting ideas together from different experiences and experiments, and being very happy when it comes out well.

SERVES 4-6
(make a big batch anyway as you can use the leftovers for salads or other dishes)

a few big handfuls of organic
    edible pet hay
2 tbsp chamomile tea flowers
vegetable oil (optional)
1kg purple potatoes
sea salt
hot mustard crème fraîche and
    chopped chives, to serve

Preheat the oven to 220°C / fan 200°C / gas mark 7.

Line a casserole dish with most of the hay and a spoonful of the chamomile flowers. I like to add a little oil at this point and very lightly fry the hay over a low heat but it's a step you absolutely don't have to follow.

Prick each of the potatoes well with a fork and add to the pot, cover with a bit more hay and chamomile flowers. Cover with the lid and bake in the oven for 30 minutes or until the potatoes can be easily pierced.

Serve hot with a side helping of hot mustard crème fraîche and chopped chives.

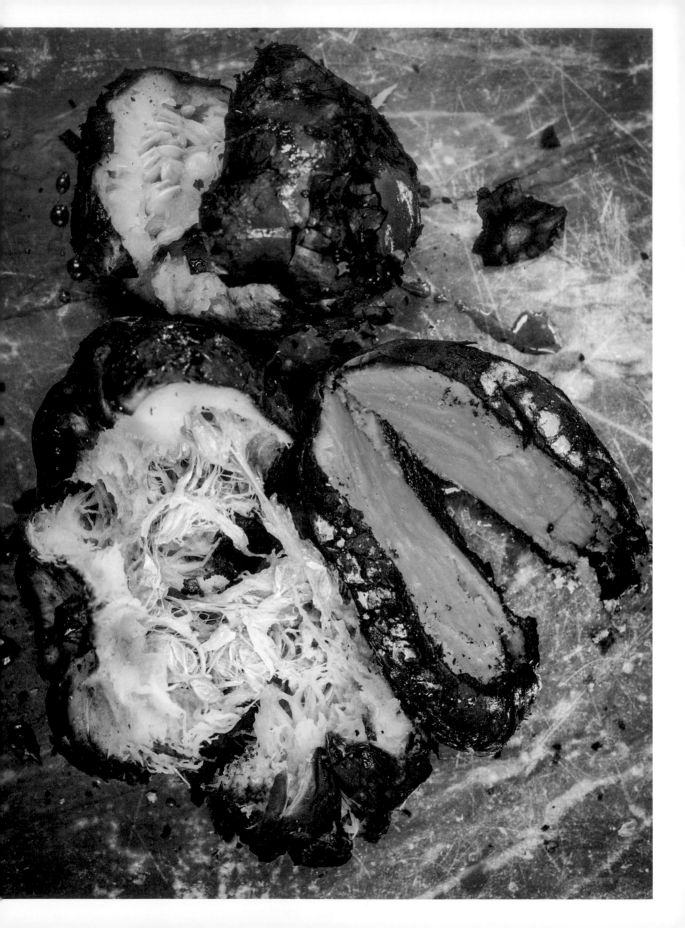

WHOLE ROASTED SQUASH

This is a very simple idea that goes back to the beginning of cooking with fire. I reminded myself about it when I bought an Egg, which is a type of ceramic barbecue, but equally you could cook like this in any type of fire that uses wood or organic charcoal – we use organic oak and hickory charcoal.

One day, I decided to throw a sweet potato and a small squash into the glowing fire, without covering them in foil. Once we could pierce them easily, we retrieved the blackened vegetables and broke them open. I just added butter and salt and we devoured the insides, working around the seeds of the squash. The flavour of the wood and smoke came straight through into the flesh – we don't eat the blackened skins. When you are outside it just connects you immediately with the nature around you, and the veg is just so good when roasted this way.

This recipe is the oven version of throwing your veg into the fire. I was cooking with a friend and put the squash into the oven whole to roast. Henry thought this was fantastic, even in its simplicity, and quickly melted together some butter, herbs and white wine vinegar. The squash announced it was ready by gently bursting at the seams and beginning to bubble. Once it had cooled a bit we scooped out the seeds and poured over the butter, scattering over lots of sea salt. This is how I would like to eat every day!

SERVES 6 as a sharing side

1.5kg squash (of any kind)
100g butter
2 tbsp white wine vinegar
2 tbsp chopped parsley
sea salt

Preheat the oven to 220°C / fan 200°C / gas mark 7. Place the squash on an oven tray and roast for about 45 minutes or until it starts to bubble through the skin.

Allow to cool and it should fall open as it rests. Scoop out the seeds.

Melt the butter over a low heat and whisk in the vinegar and parsley. Pour over the squash, scatter generously with sea salt and serve.

SMOKING, BRINING & CURING

When I have a garden I think the first thing I'll buy for it is an outdoor smoker, after I have planted a pomegranate tree and a Szechuan pepper plant. Until then I have a stove-top smoker which I bought inexpensively online and considering its humble size it gets put through its paces. It's so satisfying cooking a trout by smoking it, or smoking tomatoes to make a smoked tomato and cardamom soup.

Brining, which is simply a salt and water solution or sugar, salt and aromatics such as bay and star anise, is a great habit to get into because it is such a good way to tenderise meat. You can also use pickle juice or as I have done with the pork chop recipe in this chapter, whey water. Brining also reduces the cooking time, which then means that your meat or fish remains very moist as less heat is needed during the cooking process. It is important to remember, though, that a brine is only used once and should then be discarded.

A salt cure does more than just season. It also has a magical power to transform texture in the process. Salting wedges of savoy cabbage ahead of time lets the seasoning penetrate to the core while also tenderising the leaves. That way, when the cabbage hits the grill, it'll reach that firm-tender place on the inside before it threatens to totally blacken on the outside.

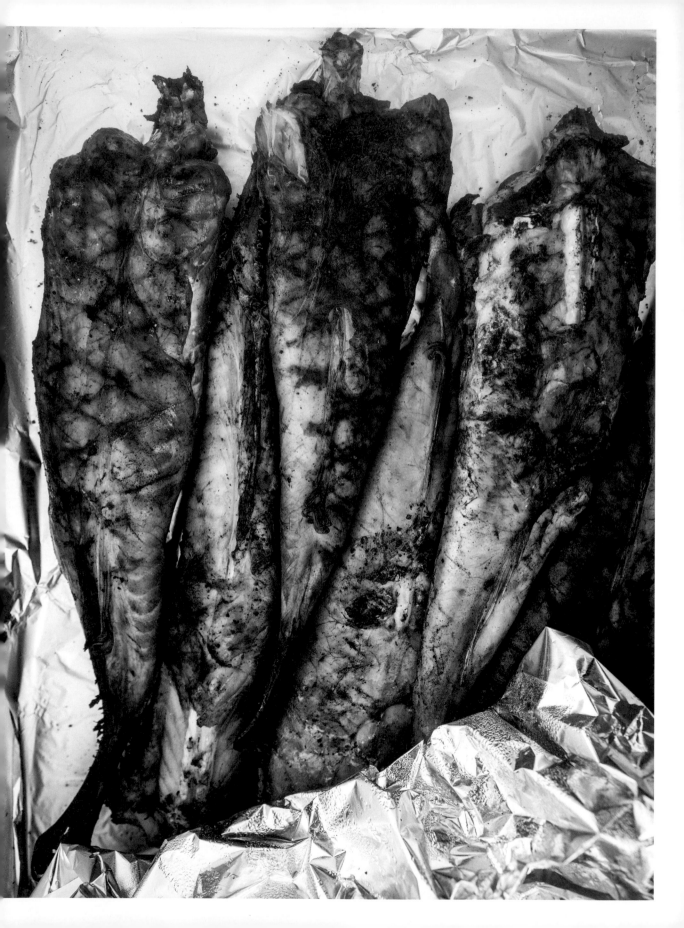

SMOKED MONKFISH WITH KIMCHI

This was the dish that stood out the most for me at our Feast of Seven Fish in Malta. This was when I went home to Malta to cook for 200 people over three days and served seven different types of fish and seafood dishes. We cured and smoked big pieces of monkfish on the bone – cooking things whole and then slicing them off the bone is always rewarding for any chef. When possible I try to replicate this kind of cooking at home, either on the hob or the barbecue. Investing in a small stove-top smoker is a clever and easy way to change the way you eat at home.

SERVES 4

1 monkfish tail
250g sea salt
250g brown sugar
peel of 1 orange
peel of 1 lime
1 tsp cloves
cherry wood chips (for the
    stove-top smoker)
4 tbsp Kimchi (page 48), to serve

Brine the monkfish tail overnight in a sealable container in the salt and sugar, citrus peel and cloves.

Before smoking, wash off the brining ingredients.

In either your home smoker or a heatproof tray lined with foil, scatter the cherry wood chips over the bottom and place the grill over them. Place uncovered on the hob over a medium heat until it starts to smoke. (Open a window!) Now place the monkfish on the grill, put the lid on the smoker or cover very tightly with foil. Lower the heat to the lowest setting and smoke the fish for 30 minutes, turning halfway through.

Remove from the heat and allow to rest and cool a little, still covered, before slicing thinly and serving with kimchi.

BBQ POUSSIN MARINATED IN FETA BRINE

You need to marinate the poussin in the feta overnight, but it does create both a tenderness and a depth of flavour that is worth the wait. This goes well with any of the salads in All I Eat is Lettuce or the Pointed Cabbage (page 115).

SERVES 2

100g barrel-aged feta (including any liquid in the packet)
4 tsp sugar
1 poussin
1 lemon, cut in half
sprig of rosemary
20g unsalted butter
crisp green salad, to serve

For the dressing
100g barrel-aged feta
50g natural yoghurt
2 tsp Dijon mustard
zest of ½ lemon
sea salt and freshly ground black pepper

Blitz the feta (excluding the 100g for the dressing) and sugar plus enough water to make into a thick smoothie consistency. Place this mixture in a pan and bring to the boil, then allow to cool.

Spatchcock the poussin – use kitchen scissors to cut along both sides of the backbone to remove it so you can then open out and flatten the poussin ready for grilling. Submerge the poussin in the feta mixture in a sealable container and leave in the fridge overnight.

When ready to cook the poussin, remove it from the brining liquid and discard the liquid. Pat the poussin dry and rub the skin with a cut lemon.

Light your barbecue and allow it to get to cooking temperature.

Lay the poussin skin side first on the hottest part of the BBQ for about 5-7 minutes, turn over and then move to the less intense heat of the outer edge. Put a cube of butter on the top of the poussin and a sprig of rosemary. If you have a lid, put this on and allow the poussin to cook until the juices run clear. It really depends on your barbecue, but this should be 20-30 minutes total cooking time.

Combine the dressing ingredients and serve with the poussin and a crisp green salad.

The alternative way of cooking this dish would be to brown the skin in a hot pan and transfer to the oven (200°C / fan 180°C / gas mark 6) for 20-30 minutes. Switch off the oven, add the butter and picked rosemary (from a sprig) and rest for 10 minutes before serving.

CURED DUCK BREAST WITH PURPLE POTATOES AND ROASTED PICKLED CHERRIES

A lot of people choose duck from the menu when they are eating out but are less confident about cooking it at home. The key part of this recipe is starting the duck breast skin-side down in a cold pan and bringing up the heat. The brining in this recipe shortens the cooking process and means the meat will be tender and flavourful.

SERVES 2

100g sea salt

100g coconut sugar

3 tsp allspice

a handful of black peppercorns

pinch of crushed red chilli flakes

2 duck breasts

200g purple potatoes (or new potatoes)

8–10 Pickled Cherries (page 42)

butter, for cooking

1 tbsp Damson Jam (page 208)

Combine the first five ingredients and place half the amount in the bottom of a plastic container. Add the duck breasts, skin-side down, then cover with the remaining spice mix. Leave overnight in the fridge.

Preheat the oven to 180°C / fan 160°C / gas mark 4.

Clean the potatoes and put in a saucepan of water, boil until cooked. Drain and season.

Meanwhile, put the pickled cherries on a baking tray, add a few little pieces of butter over the cherries and roast in the oven for about 8 minutes.

For the duck breasts, wash off the brine thoroughly and place skin-side down in a cold ovenproof frying pan. Turn up the heat under the pan. When the pan is very hot and the skin has begun to colour, turn the breasts over. After a few seconds, turn back onto the skin side and transfer to the oven for 4 minutes. Bring out of the oven and monte (see Glossary, page 14) with the fat and juices that have been released. Turn the grill on to high while you rest the duck for about 8 minutes before slicing. Drain on kitchen paper and then flash grill to warm through before serving. The resting tenderises the meat and if you have the patience is really worth it.

To serve, 'smudge' the plates with damson jam, lightly crush the potatoes and place on the plate. Scatter the roasted cherries over the potatoes before topping with the slices of duck.

LAMB NECK WITH AUBERGINE NAM PRIK

I discovered lamb neck at the school where I work while trying to use cheap cuts of really good organic meat. We do a meat pie with lamb neck and from this stemmed all the versions of brining and curing to tenderise the meat. In this recipe I cured the neck with gochujang paste, which is a spicy fermented Korean paste. Whey is also a good tenderising agent here, or brining in equal amounts of sugar and salt with a few added spices also does the trick.

SERVES 4

2 x 250g lamb neck fillets
2 tbsp gochujang paste
some lemon peel
1 garlic clove, crushed
knobs of butter, for frying
sea salt
Aubergine Nam Prik (page 52)

To brine the lamb neck fillets, rub the gochujang paste into the fillets and place them in a sealable food bag along with some lemon peel and the garlic. Seal and leave overnight in the fridge. When ready to cook, rinse and pat dry with kitchen paper.

Preheat the oven to 180°C / fan 160°C / gas mark 4.

Heat an ovenproof griddle pan to high, making sure it is really really hot, then sear the fillets for 3-4 minutes on one side. Turn over, add a couple of knobs of butter and then place the pan in the oven and cook for another 8-10 minutes. Remove from the heat, place the fillets on a board, season with a good pinch of sea salt, cover, and rest for at least 10 minutes before slicing.

Here, I have served the lamb with Aubergine Nam Prik, brought up to room temperature from the fridge larder.

HOT SMOKED SALMON

When you make hot smoked salmon at home it is softer than most of the supermarket versions you'll find. It is easier to do with a home smoker, but you can also use a foil-lined heat-proof tray – you just need to find a way to keep the smoke in as much as possible when you cover the salmon. I've used a fillet in this recipe, but it's also an amazing way to cook fish heads, once smoked you can ease away the flakes of flesh. This is delicious with Kimchi (page 48) and Whole Roasted Cauliflower (page 112). You can also make an incredible butter with flakes of the hot smoked salmon (page 57).

SERVES 2

300g salmon fillet
150g sea salt
150g brown sugar
4 cloves
4 cardamom pods, split open
rice and loose leaf chai or
    green tea, for smoking

Brine the salmon fillet in the salt and sugar, the cloves and split cardamom pods overnight in a sealable container.

Before smoking, wash off the brining ingredients and cut the fillet equally into two.

In either your home smoker or a heatproof tray lined with foil, scatter over the bottom equal amounts of rice and loose leaf chai or green tea and place the grill over the tea/rice. Place uncovered on the hob over a medium heat until it starts to smoke. (Open a window!) Now place the salmon on the grill and put the lid on the smoker or cover very tightly with foil.

Lower the heat so that the rice and tea doesn't burn and smoke the salmon for 15 minutes. Remove from the heat and allow to cool a little, still covered, before flaking and serving.

PORK IN WHEY

The importance of whey and the importance of having a hero.

I went to eat at Faviken, an incredible restaurant in the middle of Sweden that combines traditional ingredients and culture with the best of modern techniques, and met Magnus Nilsson, the head chef there. What he did not know was that I had spent the last ten years hiding in bushes and standing just close enough but not too close to him at various food events and festivals! To me, meeting Magnus was like meeting The Rolling Stones. When a mutual friend offered to introduce us I went bright red and crawled army style back to my hotel. It was nice to be an adult and still feel this way – all chefs have heroes; for me it's Magnus. David Chang is a close second, and one of the reasons why is because he started to marinate his meat in whey, the water that comes out of feta cheese, burrata or hung yoghurt. When you see the amount of lost whey in kitchens you realise why it was such a good idea to try it, and even better that it really does tenderise meat beautifully.

SERVES 2

2 pork chops (on the bone)
300ml whey (page 58)
1 tbsp olive oil
sea salt
20g unsalted butter
roasted and buttered sweet
    potatoes or Hay-Roasted
    Purple Potatoes (page 116)

Place the pork chops in a sealable bag with the whey and keep in the fridge for 1–3 hours. The meat will become increasingly tender during that time.

Strain and pat dry with kitchen paper. Bring up to room temperature, again so that the chops will remain tender on cooking.

Rub a little olive oil and sea salt into the chops. Heat a griddle pan to fairly high and place the chops on the pan. Cook for 3 minutes on each side until just cooked through. You can use tongs to hold the chops so you can crisp the fatty edge (the best bit).

Finish with a knob of butter, about a teaspoon for each chop, while allowing the meat to rest off the heat.

Serve with a little more salt and roasted and buttered sweet potatoes, or Hay-Roasted Purple Potates .

ONGLET IN DEN MISO WITH WINTER SLAW AND UMEBOSHI AIOLI

Because miso is fermented it works well to both tenderise and flavour meat. Using the Den Miso adds the extra elements of sugar and alcohol, which again helps with tenderising but also infuses the meat with Asian umami flavours.

The umeboshi plum aioli is a particularly Asian flavour, but adding a little wasabi (or horseradish) to some mayo would work well with the steak and slaw if you can't get hold of it.

SERVES 2

For the steak
250g onglet
50g Den Miso (page 55)
sea salt and freshly ground
    black pepper

For the winter slaw
1 red onion, peeled
¼ white cabbage
¼ cauliflower
2 tbsp apple cider vinegar
½ tsp grated ginger
¼ tsp grated turmeric
2 tbsp natural yoghurt

For the umeboshi aioli
1 tbsp Mayo (page 58)
1 tbsp sour cream
1 tbsp lemon juice
1 pickled umeboshi plum, stone
    removed

The day before, put the onglet in a sealable bag with the Den Miso, making sure the steak is fully covered. Seal and keep in the fridge overnight.

When ready, heat a griddle pan to a high heat and cook the meat for about 4 minutes on each side for medium rare. Take off the heat, season and rest on a board for 10 minutes.

To make the winter slaw, start by charring the onion whole in a hot grill pan or even better directly on the flame and set aside to cool.

Finely slice the cabbage and cauliflower and cooled red onion. Combine in a mixing bowl.

Heat the vinegar in a small pan with the ginger and turmeric, bring to the boil then pour over the vegetables. Finally bring all the ingredients together with the yoghurt.

To make the aioli, blend all the ingredients in a food processor until smooth.

Slice the steak and serve with the winter slaw and umeboshi aioli.

KOJI AGED RIB-EYE WITH SMOKED SALMON BUTTER AND CRISPY SALMON SKIN

Koji is a rice grain that is fermented with a live culture, similar to kefir or kombucha. It is one of the main ingredients in making soy sauce and miso but it isn't widely known about outside of Asia. However, chefs and cooks around the world are now experimenting with it and I had heard it could be used to produce a similar effect to dry ageing meat.

You can buy koji rice in Asian shops and online, and if you do try this recipe I think you will be amazed by the results. It makes the meat so tender you hardly have to cook it and gives it an extra-rich and nutty taste.

I recommend serving the steak with either Dhal (page 143) or any of the salads in this book (pages 81–97).

SERVES 4

20g koji rice (online or from an Asian/Japanese shop)
2 x 250g rib-eye steak
olive oil, for frying
10g unsalted butter
2 strips of salmon skin, optional
100g Whipped Smoked Salmon Butter (page 57)
sea salt

Blitz the koji rice in a spice blender or food processor. Place in a freezer bag with the rib-eye steaks and seal. Keep in the fridge overnight.

Before cooking, wash off the koji and pat dry with kitchen paper. Allow to come up to room temperature and season with a good pinch of sea salt on both sides.

Preheat the oven to 90–100°C / fan 70–80°C / gas mark ¼.

To make the crispy salmon skin, if using, cut it into strips and twirl it as if round a breadstick. Line a baking tray with baking paper, place the salmon strips on the paper and dry in the oven for about 1 hour until crisp.

Heat a little olive oil in a griddle over a very high heat until literally smoking hot. Lay the steaks on the griddle and cook for 1 minute on each side for rare, 2 for medium rare.

Remove from the pan onto a chopping board to rest for a couple of minutes and serve with some smoked salmon butter and a piece of crispy salmon skin.

AT THE END
OF THE DAY

Happiness and food for me seem closely connected. The day seems to come to a soft ending with a plate of food which is easy to make. Using that twenty minutes or so to put something together from the fridge is for me my unwinding - shifting gears from work mode to taking care of myself and the ones I love. When I've had a tough day it can be really therapeutic to chop vegetables and turn them into something tasty. Too many people nowadays are eating ready meals and take away because they feel that they haven't got the time to cook but they are losing something very precious. Connecting with food and taking care of yourself a little at the end of every day.

HAM, EGG AND MALTESE POTATOES

These potatoes are such a strong childhood memory of mine. Just like dipping toast soldiers into eggs, we would dip potatoes in the yolks and be happy. It's such a simple trick, but adding water to the roasting tray you use for the potatoes encourages their insides to soften while the olive oil crisps up the edges. This is a very easy dish, but often during the week it is easier to grab a ready meal than cook from scratch, so it's a little reminder of the simple things we can do to avoid that! The potatoes also go really well with a stew or Sunday roast, or a piece of pan-fried or grilled fish.

SERVES 2

olive oil, for cooking
2–3 Desiree potatoes, washed
    and thinly sliced
1 onion, thinly sliced
1 tbsp fennel seeds
1 tsp vegetable stock bouillon
    powder
4 slices prosciutto (or Home-
    cured Bacon, page 69)
2 duck's eggs (or hen's eggs)
sea salt

Preheat the oven to 220°C / fan 200°C / gas mark 7.

Oil a roasting tray and scatter the potato slices over, followed by the onion slices. Drizzle over more olive oil, sprinkle with the fennel seeds, bouillon powder and just a little salt. Add a few good splashes of water then bake for 15 minutes or until the potatoes are golden, soft in the middle and becoming crispy at the edges.

Heat a non-stick frying pan and dry fry the prosciutto until crisp. Set aside.

Using the same pan, heat a little olive oil until nice and hot and fry the eggs, sunny side up, until the whites are cooked and the yolks are still runny.

Serve the potatoes, eggs and ham together.

DHAL

I am a bit obsessed with the dhal from our local Indian restaurant and finally I managed to come up with a version at home that comes close, which is good because I could eat it at least three times a week.

SERVES 2

200g red split peas
1 tsp ground turmeric
1 tsp ground ginger
25g butter
juice of 1/2 lemon
sea salt and freshly ground
   black pepper

For the tempering
2 tbsp groundnut oil
1 tbsp cumin seeds
1 tsp chilli flakes
1 tsp black onion seeds
2 shallots, peeled and finely
   sliced

To serve
1 tsp coconut oil
100g baby spinach
sea salt

Rinse the split peas and put in a saucepan with 500ml water, the turmeric and ginger. Bring to the boil, then reduce the heat to a simmer until the lentils are breaking apart, about 20 minutes. Take off the heat and add the butter and lemon juice, giving the lentils one stir and then resting for a few minutes. Taste and season.

Heat the oil in a frying pan and add the cumin seeds, chilli flakes and black onion seeds and toss for about 30 seconds until they colour and release their aromas. Add the shallots and fry until golden. Spoon into a bowl and set aside.

In the same pan, heat the coconut oil and add the spinach and a good pinch of salt. Sauté until the spinach wilts, just a minute or so.

Serve the dhal in bowls with spoonfuls of the spiced shallots and sautéed spinach on top. A spoonful of yoghurt also works very well.

CHICKEN ON THE RACK

It's easy to forget in today's world of convenience that a roast chicken is one of the simplest and tastiest dishes to cook. Cooking any meat on the bone will give you more flavour, in this case for your vegetables, and we will usually make three meals out of a chicken, either a risotto (page 24), a salad (page 149) and soup with the stock (page 23). I know that I'm not saying anything new here, but I don't mind adding my voice to that of others when it comes to reminding ourselves about these simple things.

SERVES 2 (plus leftovers)

½ lemon
1kg free-range or organic
   chicken
600g Desiree potatoes, washed
   and sliced
400g mixed corno di toro rosso
   peppers, deseeded and cut
   in half
olive oil
sea salt
Hungarian paprika, to serve

Preheat the oven to 230°C / fan 210°C / gas mark 8.

Rub the lemon half over the skin of the chicken, then put it inside the cavity and sprinkle sea salt over the bird.

Mix the prepped vegetables with just a little olive oil and salt in a bowl and add to a roasting tray so that they are in one layer but closely touching (in other words, not spread out). Place this tray on the bottom rack of the oven, and put the chicken directly onto the rack above, breast up and tail towards the door.

Roast for 10 minutes then lower the heat to 180°C, gas mark 4 and, depending on the size of the bird, roast for about 1 hour (20 minutes per pound) until the leg juices run clear when pierced with a skewer. The vegetables will roast in the juices of the chicken that drip down.

Now tip the chicken so that any juices in the cavity are added to the vegetables. Remove the vegetable tray first, make a space in the middle for the chicken and transfer it there. Cover and rest for 10 minutes before serving.

To serve, I arrange the vegetables on the plate first, then put the chicken on top and dust the plate with a little Hungarian paprika.

CRISPY CHICKEN SKIN SALAD WITH SEAWEED MAYO

At its heart this is simply a crisp baby gem lettuce with cold roast chicken, which for me makes a perfect match. I've added an extra layer to the salad by using crispy chicken skin, as I could eat it all day. Just take it from the breasts of a whole roasted chicken then use the meat for picnic sandwiches (see below) or another dish. Anchovy, pickled seaweed or lemon zest mayo would all work well here for different variations. I made an oyster mayo, which I know won't be for everyone but it is pretty incredible.

SERVES 2

2 legs and the skin from 1 whole roasted chicken
1 tbsp Mayo (page 58)
1 tsp seaweed flakes
1 large or 2 small baby gem lettuces, leaves separated
squeeze of lemon juice
Cardamom-infused Oil (page 38), to serve
sea salt

Preheat the oven to 180°C / fan 160°C / gas mark 4.

Cut the chicken skin into bite-size pieces and lay them on an oven tray lined with baking paper. Sprinkle with salt, place another layer of paper on top and bake for about 1 hour until the skin is crisp.

Combine the mayo with the seaweed flakes and add to the lettuce leaves in two bowls along with the chicken legs and crispy chicken skin. Squeeze lemon juice over the whole dish to finish along with a drizzle of Cardamom Oil.

THE PERFECT CHICKEN SANDWICH

SERVES 2

1 skinless chicken breast, meat pulled
1/4 tsp ground turmeric
1 tsp Seaweed Mayo (see above)
1/2 baby gem lettuce, shredded
juice of 1/2 lime
sea salt
1 ciabatta loaf, sliced through the middle

In a bowl, combine the chicken meat, turmeric, mayo and baby gem. Season with lime juice and salt.

Place the mix onto one ciabatta slice and press down to allow the juices to be absorbed by the bread. Top with the other slice. Eat and enjoy.

CALVES' LIVER WITH SAGE BUTTER

This is about an 8-minute meal from start to finish that I eat every time that I crave iron. I love to simply serve with greens such as chard, kale or cavalo nero.

Learning how long to cook meat for does take practice but there are ways to use your senses instead of a timer as it so often depends on the thickness of the piece of meat you have and just the fact that each is individual. The best way I can describe it is that I know I like liver to be pink in the middle and that means it would still have 'give' when I touch it with the tongs. When it is cooked through it feels quite firm to the touch. So when you see cooking times with cooking meat on the hob do also use your own senses and judgement to get to know the feel of a steak or in this case calves' liver how you like it.

SERVES 2

500g calves' liver slices
50g butter
good handful of sage leaves
sea salt

Pat the liver dry with kitchen paper and season with a good pinch of salt on either side. Get a frying pan nice and hot and add half the butter. When it is bubbling hot, add the liver to sear on one side (don't move it around the pan, let it cook). I like it pink in the middle, which means I cook it for only about 2-3 minutes on each side, but if you prefer it to be cooked through then I would cook it for 5 minutes on each side and then have a look in the middle to check.

Throw in the sage leaves and turn the liver slices over. Cook for the same time on the other side and as you take off the heat add the rest of the butter and let the liver rest for a few minutes before serving, spooning over the melted butter and crispy sage leaves.

LOLLIPOP LAMB CHOPS

I have a collection of menus from places I have eaten all around the world over the last twenty years. Once in a while, on a rainy day, I have a look through them to see which trends have come back into cooking fashion and remind myself that there is rarely anything brand new however much we wish to be original in our ideas. One day recently I came across one of my first menus from the restaurant my father owned called Snoopy. It included spiced lamb chops with tzatziki, toasted almonds and French beans. Twenty years later I am still using the same elements which is the beauty I find in cooking – somehow through life you keep on going back to them. These are the kinds of ingredients I can rely on when I reach out with my eyes closed to create a dish.

SERVES 4

8 lamb chops, French trimmed, optional
1 tbsp coconut oil
25g Nori Butter (page 56)
200g French beans, topped and tailed
1 cauliflower
sesame oil, for coating
squeeze of lime juice
3 tbsp crushed hazelnuts
sea salt and freshly ground black pepper

For the dressing
¼ preserved lemon (or ½ if you like it extra lemony), finely chopped
30ml extra virgin olive oil
10ml white wine vinegar
sea salt

Season the lamb chops with salt, then heat a griddle pan to a high heat, add a little coconut oil and grill the chops for 2 minutes on each side, then 2 minutes again on each side, turning the chops to sear a criss-cross pattern.

Add some Nori Butter to the pan, monte (see Glossary, page 14) the chops and take off the heat to rest.

Steam the French beans for 6 minutes then refresh under cold running water to stop the cooking process and keep the bright green colour.

Make a dressing with the preserved lemon, olive oil and vinegar, plus a pinch of salt. Combine and toss with the French beans, when ready.

Slice the cauliflower into thin steaks. Put the griddle pan on a high heat and cook the cauliflower steaks for a few minutes on each side until cooked but still with a bite. Break these up, season and toss in a little sesame oil and squeeze of lime juice.

Arrange the beans on the plate first, topping with two chops each. Add some cauliflower and sprinkle over chopped hazelnuts to finish.

SEA BREAM WITH MUNG KITCHARI

This recipe is very simple and the mung kitchari makes an amazing fridge larder dish to keep on hand for a weekday evening. It might not sound incredibly appetising but it's one of those dishes that always leaves empty plates (a friend of ours gave up with his fork and used his fingers). Once you have the basic recipe you can freestyle as much as you'd like. It goes with just about anything you can think of – leftover roast chicken, pork chop, lamb, some marinated tofu or feta and most fish.

SERVES 2

For the kitchari
100g green mung beans,
    washed and soaked overnight
1 tsp ground turmeric
1 tsp nori flakes
½ tsp ground ginger
25g butter
zest and juice of 1 lemon
1 tbsp groundnut oil
6 curry leaves
1 tsp mustard seeds (or pickled,
    page 40)
1 tsp nigella seeds
1 tsp fennel seeds

For the sea bream
1 tbsp groundnut oil
2 sea bream fillets
sea salt
butter, for frying
fresh herbs, to serve

Drain and rinse the mung beans and add to a saucepan. Cover with 1 ½ times the amount of water and add the turmeric, nori flakes and ginger. Bring to the boil then reduce to a simmer, continuing to simmer for 1 hour until the beans are soft. Add the butter and a squeeze of lemon juice, give a stir and taste to see whether you wish to add a little salt. Remove from the heat and cover.

Heat the groundnut oil in a large frying pan and add the curry leaves, mustard seeds (if pickled just add to the kitchari), nigella seeds, fennel seeds and lemon zest. Allow the aromas to release in the heat and just as the seeds begin to pop, take off the heat and gently add to the kitchari, stirring through.

In the same frying pan, add a little more oil, season the fish and place skin-side down when the oil is hot. After 3 minutes, when you have good colour on the skin, turn the fillets over and add a little butter to the pan. Remove from the heat and the fish will continue to cook in the residual heat as you allow to rest for a couple of minutes.

Serve the kitchari in shallow bowls and top with the bream. Finish with a squeeze more of lemon juice and any fresh herbs you have to hand.

MONKFISH TAIL WITH FIVE-SPICE BUTTER

I think this is my favourite fish recipe. To serve, I like to sauté a few big handfuls of fresh greens in either coconut oil or butter with a scattering of sea salt, or I'll roast some halved cherry tomatoes for just a few minutes to release their flavour.

I know people are wary of monkfish because it is easy to both undercook it and overcook it, and either of these outcomes makes it hard to eat! My tip, because I really love this fish, is that after three minutes in the oven (in the recipe here) I would take the dish out of the oven and make a slit with the tip of a sharp knife down the bone. If it cuts easily and is no longer translucent this is when I just flip it and serve. If it is still a little tough or opaque in appearance I will put it back in the oven and continue to cook for a couple of minutes before checking again.

SERVES 4

2 monkfish tails
2 heaped tsp five-spice
1 tbsp coconut oil
200g cherry tomatoes
balsamic vinegar, for drizzling
50g butter
sea salt and freshly ground
    black pepper

Cut the monkfish tails in half and season. In a bowl, whisk the 5-spice with the coconut oil, rub into the monkfish and marinate for 1-2 hours.

Preheat the oven to 220°C / fan 200°C / gas mark 7.

Heat a frying pan and when very hot fry the monkfish tails for a minute on both sides to colour before transferring to an ovenproof dish and placing it in the oven for 3-5 minutes to cook through.

Place the cherry tomatoes on another oven tray and drizzle with balsamic vinegar, gently shaking the tray to make sure they are all well coated.

Remove the fish from the oven and put in the tomatoes, switching off the heat. Add the butter to a frying pan and heat until it begins to brown. Remove the tomatoes from the oven.

Spoon the butter over the fish and serve with the roasted tomatoes.

TUNA FTIRA

I decided a while back that this cookbook would be a collection of all the dishes I have cooked in different places around the world. But if I could write anything that reflects an understanding of Malta and all its flavours, it would be tuna ftira with smashed tomato, olive oil, salt and pepper. This version is made using tomato purée but smashed tomato and bread with olive oil, salt and pepper is quintessentially every Maltese person's childhood – no more, no less.

SERVES 2

1 Maltese ftira (or a large ciabatta)
extra virgin olive oil, for drizzling
1 tbsp good-quality tomato purée
150g tinned tuna, drained
1 shallot, finely chopped
1 tbsp chopped parsley
a handful of capers
10 pitted olives, chopped
sea salt and freshly ground black pepper
Giardiniera (page 47), to serve

Cut the bread in half horizontally. Drizzle the cut sides with lots of olive oil, spread with the tomato purée, season and pat together.

In a mixing bowl, put the tuna and some olive oil. Add the shallot to the bowl along with the chopped parsley, capers and olives. Mix well and taste before seasoning. If dry, add more olive oil.

Spoon the tuna mix onto one of the ftira halves, top with the other half and slice down the centre. Serve with a side of Giardiniera.

SKATE WITH XO-INSPIRED SAUCE AND CRISPY PANCETTA

Skate is a beautiful piece of fish even with a simple browning of butter in the pan while cooking the fillets. The cartilage needs to be removed, which can be done by the fishmonger.

XO is an Asian condiment which originated in Hong Kong and is made with dried scallops and dried shrimp, cured ham, chilli, oil and a combination of spices; exact recipes are usually a family secret. 'XO' translates as 'extra old', which means that you are in for something that is very special, a sauce created by the wisdom passed down through generations who have made it.

For this sauce, each ingredient is fried separately then brought together with sugar and stock. I have made a simplified version for this dish inspired by the authentic flavours.

SERVES 2

1 large skinless skate wing
20g butter
vegetable oil, for frying
salad leaves, to serve

For the XO Sauce
25g dried shrimp paste
groundnut oil, for frying
25g smoked bacon lardons
1 garlic clove
1 tsp ginger, grated
1 chilli, deseeded and and sliced
50ml chicken stock
50ml soy sauce
1 tsp brown sugar

For the crispy pancetta
6 pancetta slices

For the ginger vinaigrette, to serve
1 tbsp ginger, minced
1 tbsp rice wine vinegar
2 tbsp lime juice
200ml sesame oil

Fry the dried shrimp paste in oil first for a few minutes. The smell that comes out of this is tremendous. Transfer to the food processor. In the same pan, fry the bacon until golden brown. Add to the shrimp paste.

Fry separately the garlic, ginger and chilli, adding to the other fried ingredients when each is ready.

Pour the chicken stock into the food processor along with the soy sauce and sugar. Put on the lid, give it a shake, then let sit for 30 minutes before you pulse into a sauce. (This sauce can be kept for a month in the fridge.)

Meanwhile, cook the pancetta. Preheat the oven to 90–100°C / 70–80°C / gas mark ¼. Place the pancetta slices on a baking sheet lined with baking paper or a silicon mat and dry them in the oven for 30–40 minutes.

To cook the skate wing, melt the butter in a pan and add some vegetable oil. Place the skate fillets in the pan and cook on one side, allowing to colour. Turn and colour on the other side.

Along with the sauce and dried pancetta this is normally quite a full-on dish in flavour. A nice fresh salad with a ginger vinaigrette to accompany cuts through the heaviness of the dish: put the salad leaves in a bowl. Combine all the vinaigrette ingredients and dress the leaves. In the picture opposite I also used pineapple weed as a garnish as it cuts through the heaviness of the bacon; it is a leaf that can be foraged in the UK from May to September. A few tarragon leaves (each leaf cut in three) would also be nice.

MISO TOMATO PASTA

I once got told that as adults we just 'pretend' to love all the fancy food we order in restaurants and shop for to impress but really all we want is the food we were given as children. I hope this dish is a combination of both.

SERVES 2

1 tbsp groundnut oil
1 tbsp ground cumin
2 tbsp yellow mustard seeds
20g grated turmeric
20g grated fresh root ginger
1 x 400g can chopped
    tomatoes
50ml apple cider vinegar
20g coconut sugar
30g miso
300g fresh tagliatelle
100g cherry tomatoes on the
    vine, cut in half
handful of fresh basil leaves

Heat the oil in a frying pan and fry the cumin, yellow mustard seeds, turmeric and ginger in a saucepan for a couple of minutes until the aromas release.

Add all the other ingredients apart from the tagliatelle, cherry tomatoes and basil, and let simmer for 30 minutes–1 hour (depending on how long you can wait).

Cook the pasta in a large pan of simmering water. Drain and add to the sauce, using a bit of pasta water to loosen. Gently stir through the cherry tomatoes and most of the basil.

Serve in shallow bowls with the remaining basil leaves torn over the pasta.

FEASTING

'The ache for home lies in all of us, the safe place where we can
go as we are and not be questioned.'

Maya Angelou

During the summer months in Malta it seems as though not even a
week goes by without a feast day to celebrate one saint or another.
I wonder if that is why I am so in love with coming together and
sharing food, whether it's just for the two of us, if friends have
come over for brunch or it is a celebration. I never really put food
anywhere other than in the centre of the table. If there is a chance
for me to have friends around sitting on the floor in our living room
eating on their laps – this is me at my core.

The more time I spend away from Malta, the more I wish to return
and share all the great food discoveries I've been lucky enough to
make. During the making of this book, I did just that and returned

home to host a 'Feast of Seven Fishes'. The idea of a pop-up was quite new but we managed to find a terrace overlooking the harbour in Valletta where we could set up a long table. It's funny because I have such a romantic view of Mediterranean culture that I thought people would immediately sit next to each other and be happy to share food, but in some ways we are quite formal and it took a little bit of encouragement. Sharing bread and olive oil, yes, keep it coming throughout the meal, but sharing main courses? But the spirit of feasting won everyone over as we placed randomly sized fish caught by local fisherman on the tables along with whole roasted cauliflowers, nori buttered potatoes and flower salads. Old and new friends came to help and it was quite magical. Something very sad happened that weekend in my family that will always be intertwined with memories of the feast which sums up life for me – laughter, tears and always food.

RAS EL HANOUT SODA BREAD

Soda bread is such a great bread to make because it doesn't need any proving and is so delicious. I make this with the children at school and they are very happy when they get to take it home to show their parents or carers.

Ras el hanout is a Moroccan spice blend that you can find in most supermarkets nowadays, but you could use a sweet chilli spice instead if you prefer.

MAKES 1 SMALL LOAF

250g wholemeal spelt flour,
    plus extra for dusting
1 tsp bicarbonate of soda
1/2 tsp sea salt
1 tsp Ras el Hanout
200ml buttermilk
1 tbsp natural yoghurt, optional
Bone Marrow Butter (page 57),
    to serve

Preheat the oven to 200°C / fan 180°C / gas mark 6.

Sift the flour and bicarbonate of soda into a large bowl and add the salt and ras el hanout. Form a well in the middle and gradually pour in the buttermilk while stirring. You are looking for a soft dough, just beyond sticky. Add the yoghurt if it's a little dry.

On a lightly floured surface, knead the bread lightly for just a minute to make a loose ball. If there are cracks these make the bread lovely and crusty.

Place the dough on a floured baking tray and dust with a good amount of flour. Bake for about 30 minutes, but check the loaf sounds hollow when tapped on the bottom, as that's when it's ready.

Allow the bread to cool and serve with plenty of butter. I like to push the boat out and serve it with bone marrow butter as pictured here.

ANCHOVY TOAST WITH PICKLED ONIONS AND EDIBLE FLOWERS

The pickled onion here cuts through the anchovy perfectly. The grated cured egg is an extra hit of umami and not essential, nor are the edible flowers, of course, but they really make this the perfect way to greet any feasters.

SERVES 4 (8 toasts)

8 slices grilled baguette
extra virgin olive oil
16 fresh anchovies
16 slices Pickled Red Onions
    (page 42)
edible flowers (pags 85–6) or
    chopped fresh herbs

First, pour the olive oil into a shallow bowl. Dip one side of the toasts into the bowl and place oil side up on a plate before topping with the anchovies, pickled red onion and a scattering of edible flower petals or chopped herbs.

MACKEREL ON THE BBQ WITH YOGHURT AND DUKKAH

While we were in Malta for the pop-up feast we realised we wouldn't have enough plates to serve all the dishes. While we were over at the herb farm, Renny, the owner, overheard our conversation and went to the back of the greenhouse – and came back with a huge basketful of vine leaves for us to use instead! Thanks to the art of gentle foraging, we handed customers their mackerel on grilled vine leaves straight into their hands.

Mackerel is a wonderful fish for the grill as it is so naturally oily, the flesh doesn't easily dry out.

SERVES 6

6 mackerel fillets, seasoned
very hot wood bbq
2 tbsp Coconut Dukkah (page 66)

To serve
thick yoghurt
100g watercress
juice of 1 lemon or lime

Scatter the fillets with coconut dukkah. Grill the fillets on a hot barbecue or under the grill for 2–3 minutes, skin-side down only.

Serve immediately with thick yoghurt, watercress and a squeeze of lemon or lime.

CLAMS, SAMPHIRE AND SAKE

This is the most simple and loved recipe that I do at home for guests. Taste the samphire beforehand and then blanch accordingly to reduce the saltiness.

SERVES 4 (sharing plate)

500g clams, rinsed in cold water
1 tbsp sesame oil
small bottle of sake (180ml)
100g samphire
knob of butter
sourdough, to serve

Check the rinsed clams to make sure the shells aren't damaged and they're either tightly closed or close as soon as you give them a tap on the work surface. Discard any that remain open.

In a hot wok, add the sesame oil and let it get very hot before adding the clams. Cover and give the wok or pot a good shake.

Take off the lid and deglaze the wok with the sake. Cover again and let a few minutes pass. Now add the samphire and a knob of butter. Switch off the heat, cover and leave for a few minutes so the residual heat brings all the flavours together.

Serve in a sharing bowl with chunks of sourdough to soak up the juices.

POTATOES WITH NORI BUTTER

If you have ever been on holiday to a country on the Mediterranean you will have no doubt had grilled fish with boiled potatoes. In some restaurants the potatoes come as huge pale boulders and you wonder if you can face them, and then as you take a bite you realise they are soft but not too soft, and buttery and, somehow, just right. When I hosted the Feast of Seven Fishes in Malta I wanted to use the best of our local ingredients and add just the occasional flavour or twist learnt from my years travelling as a chef. And so for the potatoes I simply added some nori flakes to the butter, a hit with the sea-loving Maltese.

Serve alongside whole grilled fish. These are also delicious with the Calves' Liver (page 150), the Oxtail (page 196) or the Skate with XO-Inspired Sauce (page 160).

SERVES 4

500g new potatoes
50g Nori Butter (page 56) or
    50g unsalted butter with 1
    tbsp nori flakes

Boil the potatoes until soft but still with a little bite to them. Drain and return to the pan. Add the nori butter and shake the pan with the lid on to melt the butter over the potatoes.

OCTOPUS AND BABA GANOUSH

We were walking in the supermarket and came across octopus.

'No one will ever attempt to cook octopus unless they are a chef,' my wife, Kate said. This comment made me think, why do people not like to cook octopus that much? Hopefully this recipe will help to change your mind.

What restaurants achieve with octopus is not impossible to achieve at home. First, it is cooked until tender, then it is given intense heat to create a crispy, smoky caramelisation.

SERVES 8

1 chilli, whole
piece of fresh root ginger,
    peeled and sliced
5 kaffir lime leaves
1 bay leaf
1 fresh octopus (1.2kg)
Baba Ganoush (page 51)

Preheat the oven to 180°C / fan 160°C / gas mark 4.

Bring a large pot of water to the boil with the chilli, ginger, kaffir lime leaves and the bay leaf. Add the octopus, teasing it (dipping it in and out three times before submerging) and bring the water to the boil again. Cover and place in the oven for 1 hour.

Remove from the oven but let it rest in the liquid for 20-30 minutes.

Cut off the tentacles and discard the rest of the octopus. You can then create the crisp outer layer either on the barbecue or directly on the flame of your hob, or even under the grill.

This is delicious served simply with Baba Ganoush. The octopus will keep for 3 days in a sealed container in the fridge.

OCTO DOG

This is a dish that is a product of school food (not that we actually serve it to the children), an idea that was cooked up by my colleague Oli and I, and marked the start of an amazing friendship that has taken us beyond the school to pop-ups in Hackney. I promised Oli that if I make my fortune from mass-producing octo dogs we can have cocktails on every Friday after school. This dish screams fun. We often serve it on newspaper in the middle of the table with ketchup, mayo and different pickles and guests really like it.

Serving choices: either cut the Octo Dog as pictured in halves or buy small individual brioche buns. Both work well.

SERVES 8

thumb-size knob of fresh root
    ginger, peeled and roughly
    sliced
4 garlic cloves
2 bay leaves
1 tsp pink peppercorns
1 octopus (1–1.2kg)
3 big hot dog buns or 8 small
    individual brioche
1 tsp mustard powder (or hot
    mustard)
4 tbsp Mayo (page 58)
50g gherkins, cut into burnoise
100g sushi ginger, sliced
    julienne
8 toasted strips of nori,
    optional
3 spring onions, finely sliced on
    the diagonal

Preheat the oven to 160°C / fan 140°C / gas mark 3.

Add the ginger, garlic, bay leaves and peppercorns to a large pot of water and bring to the boil. Blanch the octopus in the boiling water, then take off the heat, cover and place in the oven for 2½ hours. Once cooked, let it rest for 30 minutes before draining, discarding the liquid.

Cut the buns lengthwise. Mix the mustard into the mayo and brush on the cut sides of the buns.

Cut the tentacles off the octopus and discard the body. Grill each tentacle over the flame of the gas hob, holding them with tongs until coloured on all sides. Alternatively, use a griddle pan.

Place the tentacles in the centre of the bun. Add the gherkins, sushi ginger, nori and spring onions and serve.

BEEF BRISKET IN BRIOCHE WITH BEETROOT COLESLAW

Brisket is one of those cuts of meat that needs your patience, but will reward you with amazing flavour and texture. It should become soft enough to just pull apart with a fork. I've made a brisket brioche here, but it is equally good with crushed or mashed potatoes and roasted vegetables.

SERVES 4

500g beef brisket
500g of beef stock
250ml of water
1 cascabel chilli
10g tomato paste
50ml rice vinegar
25ml balsamic vinegar
30ml soy sauce
30ml maple syrup
1tbsp sriracha sauce

To serve
4 brioche buns
beetroot coleslaw (see below)

For the beetroot coleslaw
2 medium raw beetroot, peeled and grated
1 medium carrot, grated
1 tbsp fresh grated horseradish
1 tbsp crème fraîche
sea salt, to taste
squeeze of lime juice

Combine all of the coleslaw ingredients thoroughly. Can be chilled ahead of serving.

Preheat the oven to 140°C / fan 120°C / gas mark 1.

Place the beef stock, water, chilli, tomato paste, rice vinegar and balsamic vinegar in a casserole or ovenproof saucepan, bring to the boil on the hob and whisk to combine the ingredients. Carefully add the brisket, bring back to the boil then immediately reduce the heat to a simmer.

Place in the oven for 2 hours, then remove and strain away half the liquid (you may wish to keep for soup).

Remove from the oven and with half the stock add the soy sauce, maple syrup and sriracha sauce. Bring to the boil again on the hob then transfer to the oven to cook for another hour.

Turn off the oven and allow to rest in the residual heat for an hour before serving.

To serve as brisket brioche, halve the buns and divide the brisket meat evenly, topped with beetroot coleslaw.

CRAB ARANCINI

These are a favourite of mine to serve when I want to impress – people really appreciate them and feel you have put that extra thought and effort into hosting.

MAKES 8 ARANCINI

olive oil, for frying
1 small red onion, finely chopped
250g Arborio rice
splash of Pernod
approx. 1 litre hot vegetable stock
knob of butter
2 tbsp grated Parmigiano Reggiano
100g crab meat, half white and half brown (all white if you aren't keen on brown but it does have a depth of flavour)
1 tsp wasabi paste
75g plain flour
2 eggs, beaten
150g breadcrumbs, mixed with 1 tbsp sumac and 1 tbsp black onion seeds
750ml vegetable oil, for frying
Pink Sauerkraut (page 50)
sea salt and freshly ground black pepper

Heat the olive oil in a saucepan and sauté the onion until soft and translucent. Add the rice to the pan and stir through the onion so that it is evenly coated.

Add a splash of Pernod and stir through. When it has evaporated, begin to add the hot stock in batches, stirring regularly, until the rice just has a little bite left.

Take off the heat and add a knob of butter and some Parmigiano Reggiano. Taste for seasoning. Add the crab and stir vigorously to combine. Allow to cool.

Divide the rice equally to make 8 balls.

Place the flour, egg and breadcrumb mix in separate shallow bowls. Dip each arancini ball in the flour, then the egg, and finally the crumbs, ensuring the rice is completely coated.

Pour the vegetable oil into a deep, heavy-bottomed saucepan and place over a high heat. Test the oil is hot enough by dropping in a few breadcrumbs to see if they puff up and float.

Lower the arancini into the oil, two at a time, with a slotted spoon, gently turning during cooking until golden all round. Remove from the oil and drain on kitchen paper.

Serve with Pink Sauerkraut – and prosecco, if you like.

KRUPUK QUAIL'S EGGS

In my role as a school chef I have discovered the children love quails eggs because they are so small and perfect and they are allowed to peel them for themselves. I love to offer quails eggs to friends who come for dinner as a little appetiser, even simply soft boiled. These crispy eggs, made with the same mix used for prawn crackers, are extra special. When they come out of the fryer just popped, the cracker coating puffs up full of crispiness and air, like little gifts.

SERVES 4-6

12 quail's eggs
10g raw dried prawn crackers
30g panko breadcrumbs
1/2 tsp sea salt
1 egg
50g tempura flour (or any
    other flour)
500ml vegetable oil
Lovage Chimichurri (page 54),
    to serve

Heat a pan of water, and once boiling, add the quail's eggs and cook for 2 minutes 20 seconds. Refresh and peel under cold running water so that the shell comes off easily.

Blitz the raw prawn crackers in a spice grinder, breaking them up with your hands beforehand, until you have a rough powder. Mix with the panko and salt.

Put the flour, the whisked egg and the panko/krupuk mix in separate shallow bowls. Three at a time, add the peeled eggs to the flour, then the egg mixture using one hand, then with the other hand take the egg from the egg mixture into the crumb, using the bowls to roll the mixture to fully coat the eggs.

Heat the vegetable oil in a wok (or if you have a deep fryer, use this) to 180°C and lower the eggs gently into the oil, three at a time. When golden and crisp, remove using a slotted spoon or spider and drain on some kitchen paper.

Serve all eggs in the centre of the table with a nice side of Lovage Chimichurri.

GOAT'S CHEESE GNOCCHI CARBONARA

This is quite rich but delicious if you like goat's cheese, and the gnocchi work really really well without potatoes. I keep the egg whites and make prawn toast with them, which I can always eat. (We made a Crab Toast version of this on page 29.)

SERVES 4

For the gnocchi
3 egg yolks
250g goat's cheese
90g pasta flour, plus extra for dusting
1/2 tsp (not heaped) ground nutmeg
1 tsp (not heaped) all spice

For the carbonara
olive oil, for frying
a few picked sage leaves
knob of butter
100g home-cured bacon, cut into small lardons (or lardons)
1 red onion, cut into burnoise
50ml hot vegetable stock
2 egg yolks
50g Parmigiano Reggiano, grated
fresh herbs, to serve

Whisk the egg yolks until frothy. Crumble in the goat's cheese and bash with the whisk until you have an even consistency.

Sift the flour into a bowl, make a well and add the egg-goat's cheese mixture. Combine and knead into a dough. Cut the dough in half and on a floured surface with floured hands roll each half into long sausages about 2cm diameter. Cut into bite-size gnocchi on the slant.

Bring a pan of water to the boil and reduce to a simmer. Add 8 gnocchi at a time to the water and when they rise to the top, remove with a slotted spoon and rest on kitchen paper. You can make these ahead of time and keep them in the fridge, with kitchen paper in between each layer.

To make the carbonara, heat the olive oil in a large frying pan and add the gnocchi, turning occasionally for a few minutes to heat through and colour. Add the sage leaves to the pan along with a knob of butter, remove from the heat and set aside.

In another pan, fry the lardons until they begin to colour and add the chopped onion. When caramelised, add a good splash of vegetable stock. Now add the gnocchi and sage leaves from the other pan, and toss the pan as the stock evaporates.

Take off the heat and stir through the egg yolks. Serve in bowls with ribbons of Parmigiano Reggiano and a few picked herb leaves.

RED PRAWNS

This dish and recipe comes from a lesson in gratitude for being Maltese and being surrounded by the Mediterranean Sea. Red prawns are served everywhere in summer on platters that overflow in the middle of the table. Recently friends of mine took me to a restaurant on Gozo, an island off Malta. The restaurant has only a grill on the beach and fish is caught and grilled as the day goes by. We ordered red prawns and, knowing how scarce they are in London, I forced myself to eat all the platter that was served, needing to go and swim every so often in between mouthfuls to make room! This recipe would work well with king prawns, too.

SERVES 2 (SHARING)

1 tbsp olive oil
8 red or king prawns, shells on
25ml Pernod
1 shallot, finely diced
handful of baby capers
juice of ½ lemon
knob of butter (about 25g)
chiffonade of rocket leaves,
    optional
fresh herbs, to finish, optional
slices of good bread, to serve

Heat the oil in a non-stick pan, letting it get very hot. Add the prawns, shell on, and turn gently for a few minutes until cooked. The sign that they are done is when the prawns begin to curl (or with king prawns, when they turn pink).

Deglaze the pan with half the Pernod, turn the prawns and deglaze with the remaining Pernod.

Add the shallot, capers and a squeeze of lemon. Swirl the pan, add a knob of butter and take the pan off the heat. Let the prawns rest until you can peel them.

Serve with the sauce from the pan, chiffonade of rocket and a few freshly picked anise hyssop leaves or whatever you have to hand. Serve with freshly cut bread, good for soaking up all the flavours.

CHERRYSTONE CLAMS

This dish is about presentation and simplicity. We used a Chinese bamboo steamer and served the clams on a bed of seaweed and foraged leaves.

SERVES 4

12 cherrystone clams
1 tsp finely grated fresh root
    ginger
juice of 1 lime
5 tbsp sesame oil
seaweed and leaves, to serve

Set up the steamer to have 6 clams on each tier and set it on a wok of boiling water. When you notice that the first tier of clams nearest to the water are slightly starting to open, change the tiers around.

In the meantime, add the ginger to the squeezed lime and sesame oil in a small bowl. Whisk slightly.

When the clams are all open, spoon the dressing onto each one and serve on a bed of edibles – in our case seaweed and leaves.

SALMON TAIL WITH WATERMELON AND GOAT'S CHEESE SALAD

It is a great lesson in how we eat now that a few years ago, fish tails, innards, cheeks and necks were all discarded. Now it shows off skill and that a chef cares when you find all these interior cuts done well on a menu. At home this is great once again for the centre of the table, and could be served hot or cold. Ponzu is a citrus-based Asian sauce, usually added to soy sauce. If you can't find ponzu then you can just use soy sauce here. The idea of this dish is that it is a slightly different way to serve cold salmon buffet-style in the middle of the table. You just flake away the salmon from the bone.

SERVES 4

For the salmon tail
1/2 lemon
splash of fish sauce
25ml ponzu
25ml coconut syrup, optional

For the watermelon salad
150g ash goat's cheese
300g watermelon, cut into
    cubes and deseeded
Rosemary-infused Salt (page
    39), for sprinkling
black sesame seeds, for
    sprinkling
sesame oil, for drizzling

Preheat the oven to 220°C / fan 200°C / gas mark 7.

Make diagonal cuts through the salmon skin, as shown, with a sharp knife. Rub the skin with the cut lemon and splash over the fish sauce.

Bake in a roasting tray lined with baking paper for 10–12 minutes until the skin is crispy and the flesh is soft. Rest before serving and dress with the ponzu and coconut syrup, if using.

Meanwhile, make the salad. Crumble the goat's cheese onto your serving plate. Pile the watermelon in the centre, making sure the seeds are mostly removed. Sprinkle with rosemary salt and black sesame seeds and drizzle over a little sesame oil (which has a delicious but strong taste).

PHEASANT IN MANZANILLA WITH BUTTERED ASPARAGUS, RICE AND DHAL

This idea came about because we got given a bottle of Manzanilla, so if you have a friend who brings weird bottles of alcohol to parties, please feel free to use that too. This would work really well with any sherry or port.

SERVES 4 (as a feast!)

1 pheasant
300ml Manzanilla
1 tsp pink peppercorns, crushed
olive oil, for frying
300g asparagus, woody ends snapped off
butter, for griddling
sea salt
100g cooked rice
a bowl of Dhal (page 143)

Marinate the pheasant in the Manzanilla and crushed pink peppercorns in the fridge overnight.

Preheat the oven to 200°C / 180°C / gas mark 6.

Remove the pheasant from the Manzanilla (reserving the liquid), pat dry with kitchen paper and salt. Heat some olive oil in an ovenproof casserole to a fairly high heat and sear the pheasant on all sides until the skin is golden, then turn so that the bird is breast down, add the Manzanilla back to the pot, cover and place in the oven.

Turn down the oven to 160°C / 140°C / gas mark 3 and braise the pheasant in the oven for 45 minutes–1 hour. Remove from the oven and rest for 10 minutes before serving.

To prepare the asparagus, simply cook the spears on a hot griddle pan with plenty of butter and salt.

I like to serve this with sharing bowls of boiled rice and dhal.

OXTAIL

This is one of the recipes that is especially linked to the title of this book and why I believe this title has been within me from early years. I loved oxtail as a child and would happily gnaw on the bone, and I think even now I love the meat that falls off the bone and the little fatty bits that are full of flavour.

SERVES 2 (with enough leftovers for Oxtail Strozzapreti page 199)

50g sea salt
50g sugar
850g oxtail (3 oxtails)
100ml naturally fermented dark
    Japanese soy sauce
100ml mirin
300ml chicken stock
500ml veg stock
2 shallots, skin on and halved
2.5cm piece of fresh root ginger,
    peeled and sliced
1 turnip, quartered
2 carrots, thickly sliced

The day before you want to make this dish, combine the salt and sugar and rub it into the oxtails, covering as much as possible. Place in a sealable container in the fridge and leave overnight.

Preheat the oven to 240°C / 220°C / gas mark 9.

Wash the brine off the oxtails and pat dry with kitchen paper. In a very hot pan, seal off the oxtails and deglaze the pan with soy sauce and mirin. Add the chicken and vegetable stocks, making sure the meat is covered. Add the shallots and ginger, bring to the boil, then place in the oven. After 10 minutes, lower the oven temperature to 180°C / 160°C / gas mark 4, and after another hour lower again to 150°C / 130°C / gas mark 2. Now add the remaining vegetables.

After 2 hours cooking the meat should be falling off the bone, but continue to cook at a low temperature if it needs longer to become really tender.

Rest for 10 minutes before serving each person an oxtail with some carrot and turnip and broth in bowls.

OXTAIL STROZZAPRETI

This hearty pasta is made with the leftovers from the Oxtail dish (page 196). 'Strozzapreti', the type of pasta I've used here, translates to 'Priest Strangler', as it was traditionally served to visiting clergy with butter after getting boiled in broth (the pasta, not the priest!).

SERVES 2

meat from 1 tail
250ml stock from braising the oxtail
½ of a 400g tin chopped tomatoes
300g strozzapreti
small knob of butter
1 tbsp crème fraîche

Take the meat off the bone and add it to a saucepan. Strain the stock into the pan and add the tomatoes. Bring to the boil then reduce to a simmer and cook for 10 minutes.

Using a large saucepan, boil the pasta in plenty of simmering water. Strain and add to the sauce, along with a little butter.

Take off the heat and gently combine the pasta with the sauce. Stir in some crème fraîche and serve in bowls.

TWO SPOONS
PLEASE

Puddings, pastries and desserts will always have me thinking of my sister, who in my food world has been there from the beginning. Thea was my chief tasting guinea pig during my time at culinary school and was by my side when we decided at an immensely young age to try and manage a restaurant together. She did all the baking and I cooked all the other items. This meant two main things happened – I was extremely lucky to be treated to fine banoffee and salted caramel tartlets and beautiful red velvet mini bites but also I became very lazy and hardly ever baked.

This section I dedicate to my sister and understanding that we all need to fight through our lazy patches.

XMUN BORG & SONS
BAKERY &
211 CONFECTIONERY 211

JAZZ BAR

ESTABLISHED 1906
RUBINO

CONFECTIONERY

IMPORTED SICILIAN
WINES, OILS

BOTTLED SPIRITS
SOLD HERE

LARGE
ASSORTMENT
OF
CHOCOLATE
SICILIAN C

PLATED BANOFFEE KNICKERBOCKER GLORY

Every child's recurring dream is a Knickerbocker glory. I was told once by someone older and wiser that we spend a tonne of money eating out in fancy restaurants to impress people with our vast palate but all we really want at the end is food that we used to eat as children (hence Massimo Bottura's savoury dish that is based on 'the crunchy part of lasagna').

SERVES 2

2 bananas, sliced lengthways and then cut into thirds again
25g butter
2 scoops vanilla ice cream
2 tbsp coconut crumble (see below)
1 tbsp caramel dressing (see below)

For the coconut crumble
100g flour
100g sugar
100g cold butter
40g dessicated coconut
grated zest of 1 orange

For the caramel dressing
175g light soft brown sugar
300ml double cream
50g butter
1/2 tsp sea salt

To make the coconut crumble, mix the flour and sugar in a large mixing bowl, then rub in the butter until you have a coarse breadcrumb texture. Add the coconut and orange zest and mix until thoroughly dispersed.

For the caramel dressing, combine all the ingredients in a saucepan and set over a low heat, stirring until the sugar has dissolved. Turn the heat up and bubble the sauce for 2–3 minutes until golden and syrupy. Leave to cool for 10 minutes before serving.

Heat a frying pan and melt the butter and sugar together in the pan. When it starts to bubble add the banana pieces, not turning too much so that you allow them to colour and caramelise.

To assemble, drizzle half the caramel dressing into the bottom of your bowls, then share out the caramelised bananas. Add a quenelle (see Glossary, page 14) or scoop of ice cream. Sprinkle over the crumble and drizzle over the remaining caramel.

PEACH PARFAIT WITH TURMERIC TOASTED OATS

You might wish to make a big batch of the toasted turmeric oats as it's really good to add to yoghurt and berries for breakfast or sprinkle over ice cream.

SERVES 4

400ml of prosecco
1 tsp Schezuan peppercorns
1 tsp cardamom pods, bashed
4 peaches, cut in half (stones removed)
2 tbsp runny honey
100g fresh raspberries
4 tbsp crème fraîche
4 tbsp toasted turmeric oats (see below)

For the turmeric oats
50g oats
½ tsp ground turmeric
1 tsp coconut oil
1 tsp honey

Preheat the oven to 160°C / fan 140°C / gas 3.

Mix the oats with the ground turmeric.

Heat a frying pan and add the coconut oil and honey. When hot and liquified, add to the oats in a mixing bowl and mix thoroughly.

Line a baking tray with baking paper and spread the oats out over the paper. Bake in the oven for about 30 minutes until golden and crisp. Allow to cool.

Bring the prosecco and spices to the boil, reduce to a simmer and add the peaches cut side down. Simmer for 30 minutes then remove from the heat and cover the pan. Sit until cool.

Now heat a griddle pan and place the peaches cut sides down onto the hot griddle. Drizzle over runny honey to increase the caramelisation. After a couple of minutes, when the peaches should be nicely coloured, turn over and griddle the bottoms for a minute or so.

Cut the griddled half peaches into slices and arrange in the bowls. Add fresh raspberries and a spoonful of crème fraîche on each. Scatter over some turmeric oats and serve.

BROWN BUTTER AND
SALT CUPCAKE BROWNIES

The combination of sea salt and chocolate is well known now, and it is a favourite of mine. When you add burnt butter to the mix you basically get to go to heaven.

MAKES 6

250g unsalted butter
250g coconut sugar
150g cups cacao powder
2 tsp vanilla extract
1 tsp sea salt
4 eggs
100g spelt flour
40g dark chocolate, broken
   into small pieces
crème fraîche, to serve

For the damson jam (optional)
small bowlful of freshly picked
   damsons (approx. 200g)
50ml honey

Preheat the oven to 170°C / fan 140°C / gas mark 3.

Melt the butter in a saucepan until it starts to brown, swirling it around as you heat it. Take off the heat and stir in the sugar, cacao, vanilla and salt.

Allow to cool for a few minutes and then crack in the eggs, whisking well after adding each egg until you have a shiny, thickening mixture.

Stir in the flour, mixing thoroughly into a batter.

Spoon the batter into a buttered and floured muffin tray and sprinkle over the chocolate pieces.

Bake for 15-20 minutes. You may need to test one muffin with a knife to check the middle is baked.

Remove from the oven and cool for about 10 minutes before removing from the muffin tray. You can either serve warm immediately or store in an airtight container for up to 4 days.

Here, I've served with crème fraîche and damson jam. To make damson jam, wash the damsons and warm them in a pan with a little water and honey until sticky and gooey. Keep any leftovers in a sterilised jam jar (page 37).

GINGER BEER SORBET AND APPLE JAM

Here are two quintessential flavours that I connect with Britain, apples and ginger beer. I've added spices to the simple apple jam, and you might prefer to try this without the chilli, but the heat of the flavours is a great contrast to the chill of the sorbet.

As with ice cream, keep your churning container in the freezer.

MAKES APPROX. 1L

For the sorbet
3 bottles of ginger beer (275ml)
250ml coconut milk
200g coconut sugar
1 tsp sea salt

For the apple jam
30g butter
¼ tsp ground ginger
¼ tsp ground cinnamon
¼ tsp grated nutmeg
¼ tsp chilli flakes, crushed
2 apples, peeled and diced
50g coconut sugar

Place the ginger beer and coconut milk in a pan and bring to the boil. Once boiling, whisk in the sugar and salt until dissolved. Leave to cool, then churn for about 30 minutes in an ice cream maker. Transfer to a container that you have kept in the freezer (to avoid melting). To serve use an ice cream scoop and run it under hot water beforehand.

Meanwhile, make the apple jam. In a hot pan, melt the butter and fry off the spices. Then add the apples and coconut sugar and cook until caramelised, which will be about 10–15 minutes on a low simmer (depending on your apples).

Serve the apple jam with a scoop of sorbet on top.

BEETROOT ICE CREAM

I had some beetroot powder in my spice drawer and couldn't really think what to do with it until I remembered how great beetroot is as an unusual dessert ingredient. So I got out the ice cream maker and added the beetroot to a vanilla base. Adding that hint of sweet vegetable really works.

When using an ice cream maker you need to put the bowl into the freezer a day ahead. You can use an electric mixer if you don't have an ice cream maker, just whisk a couple more times while the ice cream is freezing to get as much air into the mixture as possible. And freeze your container first too using either method.

Recently I had sourdough ice cream in a restaurant in Sydney, Australia. It was such a clever and delicious way to use up leftover bread and had an amazing sweet saltiness. Once you have a basic ice cream recipe you like to use (with or without egg yolks) you can really experiment with flavours.

MAKES APPROX. 600G

180ml whole milk

75g brown sugar

pinch of sea salt

2 heaped tsp beetroot powder
  (available online and in
  natural heath food shops and
  spice shops)

1/2 vanilla bean

3 egg yolks

300g double cream

waffle cone and seaweed
  flakes, to serve

Combine the milk, sugar, salt and beetroot powder in a saucepan. Split the vanilla bean lengthwise and scrape the seeds from one half into the saucepan along with the other ingredients. Bring to the boil and then remove from the heat and cover. Allow to cool for about 30 minutes.

Beat the egg yolks in a mixing bowl. Re-heat the milk mixture and slowly pour into the beaten eggs, whisking all the time. The mixture should thicken nicely.

Strain this mixture into another bowl containing the double cream.

Cover with clingfilm and chill overnight or if you don't have time to wait place in the freezer to cool until chilled.

Process in an ice cream maker for about 20 minutes until good and thick then transfer to your container (a loaf tin lined with greaseproof paper is good) and freeze for a couple of hours.

Here, I've simply served in waffle cones with a few dulse seaweed flakes sprinkled over.

SEAWEED SALTY BARK AND CHAMPAGNE

This is really simple but people can't keep their hands off it and it's a nice way to add a homemade touch to chocolate. The seaweed was a gamble but it works so well. Other ingredients I've tried include a mix of toasted pumpkin, sunflower and hemp seeds, rosemary, dried cherries and toasted pecans.

MAKES 6–8 SHARDS

200g dark chocolate
2–3 heaped tbsp dulse
    (seaweed) flakes
a few good pinches of sea salt
Pickled Cherries (page 42),
    to serve

Place a heatproof bowl over a saucepan with water in the bottom (but not touching the base of the bowl). Bring the water to a gentle simmer and break the chocolate into the bowl. Use a spatula to stir the chocolate until completely melted and smooth.

Line a baking tray with greaseproof paper and pour the melted chocolate onto the paper, spreading it as evenly as possible using the spatula

Sprinkle over the seaweed flakes and salt. Transfer to the fridge to cool for at least a couple of hours.

To serve, break the 'bark' into shards. I serve these with pickled cherries – and a glass of champagne!

INDEX

ABOUT THE AUTHOR

Nicole Pisani is a chef who has worked at Yotam Ottolenghi's restaurant NOPI and Anna Hansen's The Modern Pantry in London. Before that she ran a family restaurant in Malta, where people still stop her in the street to tell her how much they miss her cooking.

Always happy to take on a challenge and always happy to feed people, Nicole now runs a school kitchen and food education programme in Hackney after answering a tweet from Henry Dimbleby, co-founder of LEON restaurants and co-author of The School Food Plan, asking if anyone knew a chef who would be interested in cooking at his children's community primary school.

Nicole's first cookbook *Magic Soup* was published in 2015 by Orion Books.

'Nicole is smart and generally brilliant' Yotam Ottolenghi

THANK YOU

Kate Adams (co-author in books and life)

Emma Diacano, Pierre Malouf, Andrew Cutajar, Chery-Lynn Booth and my beautiful sister Thea Pisani Fraser for the feast in Malta. And to Oliver Pagani for the octodog and for being part of who I am as a chef currently.

Amanda Harris for seeing the glitter, Emily Barrett, Helen Ewing and Mark McGinlay at Orion / Seven Dials and our literary agent Clare Hulton.

Thank you to Regula Ysewijn for the stunning photographs.

A Note on Sustainable Fish

When photographing this book the fish we used was from local fisherman in Malta Cornwall and a reputable fishmonger in London. The list of sustainable fish changes from year to year and also depends on the individual fishing practices.

First published in Great Britain in 2018 by Seven Dials
An imprint of Orion Publishing Group Ltd
Carmelite House, 50 Victoria Embankment, London, EC4Y 0DZ
An Hachette UK Company

10 9 8 7 6 5 4 3 2 1

Text © Nicole Pisani 2018

A CIP catalogue record for this book is available from the British Library.

Hardback ISBN: 9780297608868

Photography: Regula Ysewijn
Design and illustrations: Caroline Clark Design
Props: Tamzin Ferdinando
Food styling: Nicole Pisani

Printed and bound in China

The Orion Publishing Group's policy is to use papers that are natural, renewable and recyclable products and made from wood grown in sustainable forests. The logging and manufacturing processes are expected to conform to the environmental regulations of the country of origin.

www.orionbooks.co.uk

For more delicious recipes plus exclusive competitions and sneak previews from Orion's cookery writers visit **kitchentales.co.uk**